THE
TAMING OF THE SHREW

By
WILLIAM SHAKESPEARE

With Commentaries and Glossaries
by
George Skillan

SAMUEL FRENCH, INC.
45 WEST 25TH STREET   NEW YORK 10010
7623 SUNSET BOULEVARD HOLLYWOOD 90046
LONDON   TORONTO

A NOTE

The intention of this edition of The Taming of the Shrew is to catch something of the spirit of an Elizabethan presentation of the play.

Whilst not strictly conforming to a presentation in an Elizabethan Playhouse it is possibly something akin to the Strolling Players' method when performing in a patron's mansion.

The audience is intended to view the play through the bemused eyes of Sly, and producers should keep this in mind and, according to their individual ideas, can introduce by-play between Sly and the actors of the play proper that will keep the spectators in touch with this idea. The play should be spoken rapidly and lightly. The actors should not take it seriously. Much of the rough and vulgar business so long associated with the play can be omitted with advantage to the comedy.

Costumes of the Elizabethan period should be used.

FOREWORD

The Taming of the Shrew is one of the happiest of Shakespeare's comedies. It has romance, frolic and studied dramatic development in the main theme which, though so delightfully seasoned with buoyant comedy, has a clear and disciplined career in the conflict of two real people.

In all his work Shakespeare could never cease from being an artist. There was always principle, self-government in whatever he wrote. It came from his inner being whether as a throe of tragedy, a throb of love, or a whim of humour. Fundamentally, in each different manifestation the pattern is the same, the issue fine with balance, contrast in technical construction, and a temperance which gives the spasms of most powerful passion or the exuberance of leaping delight a conviction of reality.

It is sometimes difficult to realize the processes that hide in the natures of simple things and preside in their operation. A wavelet twinkling on the easy bosom of the sea has infinite origin with the moon as sponsor and the sun as priest in its baptism of light. The bitter strength of winter's severities smile in the first snowdrop, and the spritely and light harmonies of the morning bird chorus are the colloquial transpositions of nature's first giant music in the assembling and blending of her elements. These are not poetical fallacies but organic facts : and the true artist repeats the process in his work : he cannot help it ; he is a part of creation. There is a great difference between a deeply wise man in what he says and does, and the straining contortions of egotistical cleverness ; between one of nature's gentlemen and the sycophant ; between the easy humour of a man happy in realities and the tricky wit of smart sophistication.

This may seem quite inapposite to an introduction to a Shakespearean comedy, but its growth is from the same source and is of the same substance as his grand emotions and disasters of life ; and, like them, it shows the same beauty of movement in its slighter way.

It is, unfortunately, a not infrequent custom in these days to exchange delicacy of character, situation and event for slapstick and farce. Comedy of life becomes absurdity of burlesque and the richness of real amusement is squandered in unrighteous nonsense. Shakespeare has bigger resources than that, and it is a low ambition to discredit him in such a trivial way. The people are unreal and so are the circumstances the moment the style violates nature. Shakespeare is always an artist of life bringing bold minds into contact and even conflict, without clumsiness. This is the basic design of his work ; and when a coarse distortion is imposed by insensitive production and acting, the intruder quarrels with the master of the house and there is a friction. To the judicious, the operation aches, whilst the unskilful laugh. Let the necessary question of the finer considerations of the Poet possess the imagination and have its way.

In the appended commentaries an effort has been made to guide the reader to see the more prominent points of direction towards the proper realization of the true nature of the play. It is not easy to summarize a scene in all its particular essentials without confusing the reader with too much detail, but it is hoped that such necessities as are required to keep the refined principles in operation have been sufficiently indicated, to prompt the reader into more extensive application of them throughout the scenes. Given a fair artistic treatment, this play can always be young and fresh with its own unique life and entertaining qualities, a thing of natural poise and behaviour and charm, graces which vanish beneath the galvanic shocks of trick and sophistication.

SHAKESPEARE'S USE OF LANGUAGE

To the Elizabethan, language had a greater significance than it has to the modern man ; for in that remarkable social change which took place as the result of Richmond's victory at the battle of Bosworth, a change which was great and deep enough to give birth to Modern England, men found not only domestic liberty but spiritual freedom as well ; and language, more than any other gift, is the greatest means both of intercourse and expression of mental and spiritual assertiveness. The life of men is in their souls, and true life does not grow by accretion from without, but by change of condition from within; and by exercising character from within outwards, their works become creative and are revelations of their own great and fundamental nature : and what human faculty can be more creative or revealing or expressive of man's infinite capacity than language ? Words determine more than anything else in the traffic of human progress, or, unfortunately, human disaster.

The two great manifestations of these facts at this period of rebirth were the translation of the Bible into English, and Shakespeare. In the one we had the re-presentation of the language in its most powerful literal and factual form, and in the other the manifestation of its full dramatic capabilities, that is, the ability to awaken the imagination into the experience of things, by emotional-enactment in sound. Language being a wider acquisition under the evolutionary process of spiritual-cultural emancipation, the fact that Shakespeare's English is the colloquial, not the academic or precise literary English of his day, shows its elevation as a public commodity of the time, for he, like all sons of greatness, spoke in a language that all men could understand. He was the product of circumstances which reveal that the colloquial English of the period was an object of great concern and care, and not the reduced medium of convenience of the present day. It came from a depth of the profound liveliness of a new condition of being; and producers and actors who try to treat Shakespeare's words with the triviality of modern usage fail to realize that they are victimizing them under a vice of the present times and not accommodating them with a virtue; and that the Elizabethan, as natural a man as any today, did not throw his words away : they were too precious as the redeeming elements of his new liberty.

As insufficient as the above comments may be, they will enable attention to be focussed upon the need for respecting the words of Shakespeare before any ripe action is possible : for his words are developed only by their union with their fellows, in the same way that colour develops colour, or one note of music is given its secret value by another. Four notes played singly reveal very little in combination they create music. The words that make up the celebrated ' Mercy Speech ' in *The Merchant of Venice* are such as, dispersedly, we use a hundred times or more in the course of our day's speaking, without realizing any remarkable eloquence. Yet, in one particular composition they are presented in indelible worth. But the actor has to do his share in the achievement of this metamorphosis ; ' it is not enough to speak, but to speak *true* '. He must exercise his words with artistic discretion before the process of connotation (that is the combining of elementary word sounds, in order to develop a mutual, additional quality) can have its perfect work.

A further advantage gained by this emancipation of words is that it enables them clearly to indicate the kind of treatment that is required for specific passages. They announce the necessary style to be adopted and the various changes of that style, without which monotony will corrupt even the best conscientious ' feeling ' of the drama or poetry. These changes vary into the rhetorical, colloquial or purely declamatory methods of treatment, in matter of pace or other distinctions that enable the pitch to be relaxed without losing the grip, and climaxes to be avoided before their proper time. Once the active nature of words are liberated, they will dictate these essential elements of flexibility and variety without which no work of art in any form can respond to its parent inspiration : for the action must never become ' weary, stale, flat and unprofitable '; if it does it will soon die.

Among the many things that must otherwise be left unsaid, one negative instruction is of the greatest importance; and that is that pace and sheer noise alone are of no value. Here again, if the words are properly and fully developed, and if they are governed by the rise and fall of proper modulation, their own active natures—and they will always be found very true to their dramatic purpose—will provide both animation and power without either undue hurry or over-strain of voice. Never rush the words so that they become mere sounds signifying nothing; never blast them beyond their instrumental capacity. It is their articulate performance that enables them to be fruitful ; and if this is not guarded by strict discipline, the actor will rob himself of the very effect at which he is aiming.

After the proper attention to the words, study to vary the treatment in the different sections of the scenes, and even in speeches, yes, and sometimes in different sections of single lines, so as to preserve the values by variation either of pace, intensity or mood.

DRAMATIS PERSONÆ

INDUCTION

A LORD.

CHRISTOPHER SLY . . . . A Tinker.

TWO HUNTSMEN.

FOUR SERVANTS.

BARTHOLOMEW . . . . (Page as a Lady.)

PAGES.

HOSTESS.

PLAYERS

BAPTISTA . . . . A gentleman of Padua.

VINCENTIO . . . . A merchant of Pisa.

LUCENTIO . . . . Son to Vincentio.

PETRUCHIO . . . . A gentleman of Verona.

GREMIO
HORTENSIO } . . . . Suitors to Bianca.

TRANIO
BIONDELLO } . . . . Servants to Lucentio.

GRUMIO
CURTIS } . . . . Servants to Petruchio.

A PEDANT.

OTHER SERVANTS TO PETRUCHIO.

FOUR PLAYER BOYS.

BOY FOR LOCATION CARD.

GUESTS (MALE AND FEMALE).

KATHARINA
BIANCA } . . . . Daughters to Baptista

A WIDOW

GUIDE TO SCENES

PART I

GUIDE TO SCENES (*continued*)

PART II

Full Scene.	*I	Petruchio's House.
Traverse No. 1 or 2	*II	Near Baptista's House.
Full Scene.	III	Petruchio's House.
Traverse No. 2.	*IV	Before Baptista's House.
Traverse No. 2.	*V	A Public Place.
Traverse No. 2.	*VI	Before Lucentio's Lodging.
Full Scene.	VII	Lucentio's House.
Traverse No. 1.	VIII	Epilogue.

* Denotes where Location Cards are used.

FURNITURE AND PROPERTIES

PART I

FURNITURE.

Divan or bed for Sly.
Table by bed. (That used in last scene.)
Chair by bed.
Chairs for Lord, Sly, and others according to numbers.
Arbour.

PROPERTIES.

Goblets.
Flagons.
Dish with conserves.
Washing basin.
Napkin.
Musical Instruments.
Bundle of books.
Whip (Petruchio.)
Whip (Grumio.)
Bouquets { Katharina. / Bridesmaids.
Bundles for Players.
Boys to carry in Induction entrance.
Cap for haberdasher.
Gown } For Tailor.
Yard }

LOCATION CARDS.

Before Hortensio's House.
Before Baptista's House.
Baptista's House.
Baptista's Garden.
Petruchio's House.
Near Baptista's House.
A Public Place.
Before Lucentio's Lodging.

PART II

FURNITURE.

Large oak table.
Small do. (as used for Sly).
6 oak chairs.
4 stools or meaner chairs.
Fire represented by logs on a stone slab.
Bench.
Tables and chairs used in Petruchio's house can be used again in last scene.

PROPS OFF STAGE.

2 knives.
2 forks.
Carving knife and fork.
2 platters.
Dish with meat on it.
Cover for same.
2 goblets.
Flagon.
Washing bowl.
Goblets, flagons, etc., as in Part I.

COSTUME PLOT

PERIOD ELIZABETHAN

SLY	1st and 3rd, Ragged and dirty suit. 2nd, Rich sleeping attire. Rich overgown. Slippers.
THE LORD	Rich hunting attire.
HUNTSMEN	Hunting attire (uniform).
FOUR SERVANTS	Uniform
PLAYERS	For Induction entrance the players can be top-booted, rough-hatted, with large rough cloaks covering their " play " costumes.
BARTHOLOMEW (PAGE)	Seen only in rich ladies' attire.
LORD'S PAGES	Uniform.
BAPTISTA	Middle-aged rich attire. Breeches, surcoat. Can have change of surcoat and collar for marriage scenes.
VINCENTIO	Middle-aged rich attire. Dressed for travelling.
LUCENTIO	1st. Rich travelling attire. 2nd. Long disguise gown, cap. 3rd. Rich suit
PETRUCHIO	1st. Rich, but strong travelling attire. 2nd. Fantastic ragged attire. (Text will guide.) 3rd. Rich attire.
GREMIO	Old dandy of the period.
HORTENSIO	1st. Plain but good attire. 2nd. Long disguise gown, cap. 3rd. Rich attire.
TRANIO	1st. Well-dressed servant. 2nd. Rich attire.
BIONDELLO	Servant's attire.
GRUMIO	1st. Servant's attire. 2nd. Fantastic ragged attire. (See text.)
CURTIS	Servant's attire.
PEDANT	1st. Rather threadbare elderly attire. Surcoat. 2nd. Dressed as Lucentio's father.
PETRUCHIO'S SERVANTS	Varied servant's attire.
PLAYERS' BOYS	Simple but bright attire.
KATHARINA	1st. Rich young lady. 2nd. Wedding dress. 3rd. Torn and dirty double of wedding dress. 4th. Rich travelling attire.
BIANCA	Rich young lady.
WIDOW	Rich attire.
LADY GUESTS	Varied.

NOTE. Elizabethan gentlemen *always* wore—or carried in hand or belt—gloves.
Make collars and ruffs as varied as possible.
When travelling, Elizabethan ladies and gentlemen covered up their fine clothes with large cloaks.
Vary the hats. Pots and flats.

L.L. Oak flats.

K.K. Oak flat with large opening.

M.M. Rostrums with steps.

G.G. Small oak fats with return pieces. (" Book " wings can be used.)

F.F. Practical door pieces with balconies and window above. Return pieces above and below.

H.H. Traverse No. 2, i.e. curtains to draw across stage opening and meeting c.

E.E. Traverse No. 1. Ditto.

D. Act drop or main curtain.

C.C. Proscenium wings with entrances.

B.B. Proscenium.

A.A. Apron—or forestage.

Note. If there is no forestage the space between Act drop and Traverse 1 may be used.

Traverse 1 should be so arranged as not to shut out Sly, Lord and characters viewing the play. The producer must use Traverse 2 instead of 1 if space will not permit the use of the latter.

The scene should represent a Hall in an Elizabethan Mansion. Traverse should work R. and L. from c. The whole setting may be devised with curtains. All directions to be read as from the stage; the actors right and left, etc.

THE TAMING OF THE SHREW

THE INDUCTION

SCENE I [1]

Near the LORD'S *house.*

Enter L. SLY *and* HOSTESS *arguing.*

SLY. [2] I'll pheeze you, in faith.

HOSTESS. [3] A pair of stocks, you rogue !

SLY. Ye are a baggage : the Slys are no rogues ; look in the chronicles ; we came in with Richard Conqueror. Therefore *paucas pallabris* ; [4] let the world slide : [5] *sessa* [6]

HOSTESS. [7] You will not pay for the glasses you have burst ?

SLY. [8] No, not a denier. Go by, Jeronimy : go to thy cold bed, and warm thee.

HOSTESS. I know my remedy ; I must go fetch the third-borough.

[*Exit* L.

SLY. Third, or fourth, or fifth borough, I'll answer him by law : I'll not budge an inch, boy : let him come, and kindly. [*Falls asleep.*

Horns winded. Enter R. *a* LORD *from hunting, with his train.* [9]

LORD. [10] Huntsman, I charge thee, tender well my hounds :
Brach Merriman, the poor cur is emboss'd ;
And couple Clowder with the deep-mouth'd brach.
Saw'st thou not, boy, how Silver made it good
At the hedge-corner, in the coldest fault ?
I would not lose the dog for twenty pound.

FIRST HUNTSMAN. Why, Belman is as good as he, my lord ;
He cried upon it at the merest loss
And twice to-day pick'd out the dullest scent :
Trust me, I take him for the better dog.

LORD. Thou art a fool : if Echo were as fleet,
I would esteem him worth a dozen such.
But sup them well and look unto them all : [11]
To-morrow I intend to hunt again.

FIRST HUNTSMAN. I will, my lord. [12]

LORD. [13] What's here ? one dead, or drunk ? See, doth he breathe ?

SECOND HUNTSMAN. He breathes, my lord. Were he not warm'd with ale,
This were a bed but cold to sleep so soundly.

LORD. O monstrous beast ! how like a swine he lies !
Grim death, how foul and loathsome is thine image ! [14]
Sirs, I will practise on this drunken man.
What think you, if he were convey'd to bed,
Wrapp'd in sweet clothes, rings put upon his fingers,

1

A most delicious banquet by his bed,
And brave attendants near him when he wakes,
Would not the beggar then forget himself ?

> FIRST HUNTSMAN.[1] Believe me, lord, I think he cannot choose.
> SECOND HUNTSMAN.[1] It would seem strange unto him when he waked.
> LORD. Even as a flattering dream or worthless fancy.

Then take him up and manage well the jest:
Carry him gently to my fairest chamber
And hang it round with all my wanton pictures:
Balm his foul head in warm distilled waters
And burn sweet wood to make the lodging sweet:
Procure me music ready when he wakes,
To make a dulcet and a heavenly sound ;
And if he chance to speak, be ready straight
And with a low submissive reverence
Say *What is it your honour will command ?*
Let one attend him with a silver basin
Full of rose-water and bestrew'd with flowers ;
Another bear the ewer, the third a diaper,
And say *Will't please your lordship cool your hands ?*
Some one be ready with a costly suit
And ask him what apparel he will wear ;
Another tell him of his hounds and horse,
And that his lady mourns at his disease :
Persuade him that he hath been lunatic ;
And when he says he is, say that he dreams,
For he is nothing but a mighty lord.
This do and do it kindly, gentle sirs :
It will be pastime passing excellent,
If it be husbanded with modesty.

> FIRST HUNTSMAN. My lord, I warrant you we will play our part,
As he shall think by our true diligence
He is no less than what we say he is.
> LORD. Take him up gently and to bed with him ;
And each one to his office when he wakes.

[*Two* HUNTSMEN *bear out* SLY.[2] *A trumpet sounds* R.

Sirrah, go see what trumpet 'tis that sounds :

[*Exit* SERVINGMAN R.

Belike, some noble gentleman that means,
Travelling some journey, to repose him here.

Re-enter SERVINGMAN R.

How now ! who is it ?

> SERVINGMAN.   An't please your honour, players
That offer service to your lordship.
> LORD. Bid them come near.

Enter PLAYERS.[3]

Now, fellows, you are welcome.

> PLAYERS. We thank your honour.
> LORD. Do you intend to stay with me to-night ?
> A PLAYER.[4] So please your lordship to accept our duty.
> LORD. With all my heart.[5] This fellow I remember.

Since once he play'd a farmer's eldest son :
'Twas where you woo'd the gentlewoman so well :

---

[1] *Laughing.*

[2] *If company allows other attendants can carry* SLY, *in which case they should enter with the rest.*

[3] *Here enter all players concerned in the play proper. Some carry bundles. They stand in group R.C. LORD C.*

[4] *The* PLAYER *of* BAPTISTA.

[5] *Pointing to the* PLAYER *of* PETRUCHIO.

I have forgot your name; but, sure, that part
Was aptly fitted and naturally perform'd.
    A PLAYER.[1] I think 'twas Soto that your honour means.
    LORD. 'Tis very true: thou didst it excellent.
Well, you are come to me in happy time;
The rather for I have some sport in hand
Wherein your cunning can assist me much.
There is a lord will hear you play to-night:
But I am doubtful of your modesties;
Lest over-eyeing of his odd behaviour,—
For yet his honour never heard a play—
You break into some merry passion
And so offend him; for I tell you, sirs,
If you should smile he grows impatient.
    A PLAYER. Fear not, my lord: we can contain ourselves,
Were he the veriest antic in the world.
    LORD.[2] Go, sirrah, take them to the buttery,
And give them friendly welcome every one:
Let them want nothing that my house affords.

        [Exit an attendant with the PLAYERS.[3]

Sirrah,[4] go you to Barthol'mew my page,
And see him dress'd in all suits like a lady:
That done, conduct him to the drunkard's chamber ·
And call him *madam*, do him obeisance.
Tell him from me, as he will win my love,
He bear himself with honourable action,
Such as he hath observed in noble ladies
Unto their lords, by them accomplished:
Such duty to the drunkard let him do
With soft low tongue and lowly courtesy,
And say *What is't your honour will command,*
Wherein your lady and your humble wife
May show her duty and make known her love?
And then with kind embracements, tempting kisses.
And with declining head into his bosom,
Bid him shed tears, as being overjoy'd
To see her noble lord restored to health,
Who for this seven years hath esteemed him
No better than a poor and loathsome beggar:
And if the boy have not a woman's gift
To rain a shower of commanded tears,
An onion will do well for such a shift,
Which in a napkin being close convey'd
Shall in despite enforce a watery eye.
See this dispatch'd with all the haste thou canst:
Anon I'll give thee more instructions.

        [Exit a SERVINGMAN.L.

I know the boy will well usurp the grace,
Voice, gait and action of a gentlewoman:
I long to hear him call the drunkard husband,
And how my men will stay themselves from laughter
When they do homage to this simple peasant.
I'll in to counsel them; haply my presence
May well abate the over-merry spleen
Which otherwise would grow into extremes.

        [Exeunt L., *followed by attendants.*

[1] PETRUCHIO.

[2] *To an attendant who stands on his* L.

[3] *All cross stage to* L. *and bow to* LORD *as they go.*
[4] *To another attendant.*

SCENE II

The LORD'S *house.*

Business of SLY *waking.*

Main curtain rises, if last scene is played on forestage, or traverse opens if not, discovering SLY *in bed (or on a couch).*
The LORD *is standing* L.C. *watching* SLY.
FIRST SERVANT *standing* R. *of bed.*
SECOND SERVANT *standing below him.*
THIRD SERVANT *standing* L. *top.*
PAGE *masquerading as wife is being dressed by two pages* L.C. *at back.*
A table stands R. *of bed on which are dishes, drinking cups, washing bowl, etc.*
Apparel for SLY *on chair* L. *of bed.*
Musicians in balcony R. *If no balcony, grouped conveniently.*
Seats ready in balcony L. *for* SLY *and party. If no balcony, arrange seats* L. *down stage.*

SLY.[1] For God's sake, a pot of small ale.

FIRST SERVANT.[2] Will't please your lordship drink a cup of sack ?

SECOND SERVANT.[3] Will't please your honour taste of these conserves ?

THIRD SERVANT. What raiment will your honour wear to-day ?

SLY.[4] I am Christophero Sly ; call not me *honour* nor *lordship* : I ne'er drank sack in my life ; and if you give me any conserves, give me conserves of beef.[5] ne'er ask me what raiment I'll wear ; for I have no more doublets than backs, no more stockings than legs, nor no more shoes than feet ; nay, sometime more feet than shoes, or such shoes as my toes look through the overleather.

LORD.[6] Heaven cease this idle humour in your honour !
O, that a mighty man of such descent,
Of such possessions and so high esteem,
Should be infused with so foul a spirit !

SLY.[7] What, would you make me mad ? Am not I Christopher Sly, old Sly's son of Burton-heath, by birth a pedlar, by education a card-maker, by transmutation a bear-herd, and now by present profession a tinker ? Ask Marian Hacket, the fat ale-wife of Wincot, if she know me not : if she say I am not fourteen pence on the score for sheer ale, score me up for the lyingest knave in Christendom. What ! I am not bestraught : here's—

THIRD SERVANT.[8] O, this it is that makes your lady mourn !

SECOND SERVANT.[8] O, this is it that makes your servants droop !

LORD. Hence comes it that your kindred shuns your house,
As beaten hence by your strange lunacy.
O noble lord, bethink thee of thy birth,
Call home thy ancient thoughts from banishment
And banish hence these abject lowly dreams.[9]
Look how thy servants do attend on thee,
Each in his office ready at thy beck.[10]
Wilt thou have music ? hark ! [11] Apollo plays

[*Music.*

And twenty caged nightingales do sing :
Or wilt thou sleep ? we'll have thee to a couch
Softer and sweeter than the lustful bed
On purpose trimm'd up for Semiramis.[12]
Say thou wilt walk ; we will bestrew the ground.
Or wilt thou ride ? thy horses shall be trapp'd,

[1] *Coughing.*
[2] *Advancing with cup.*
[3] *Advancing with dish.*

[4] SLY *looks at them wonderingly.*

[5] *Servants place cup and dish back on table, laughing as they turn from* SLY.

[6] *Advancing to* SLY.

[7] *Standing up on bed.*

[8] *Taking* SLY *by the hand and coaxing him to lie down.*

[9] SLY *has been coaxed down and the servants are bowing.*

[10] *Signing to Musicians.*
[11] *Music.*

[12] *During this speech the* SERVANTS *indulge in silent laughter, hiding their amusement from* SLY.

Their harness studded all with gold and pearl.
Dost thou love hawking? thou hast hawks will soar
Above the morning lark: or wilt thou hunt?
Thy hounds shall make the welkin answer them
And fetch shrill echoes from the hollow earth.

FIRST SERVANT.[1] Say thou wilt course; thy greyhounds are as swift
As breathed stags, ay, fleeter than the roe.

SECOND SERVANT.[1] Dost thou love pictures? we will fetch thee straight
Adonis painted by a running brook,
And Cytherea all in sedges hid,
Which seem to move and wanton with her breath
Even as the waving sedges play with wind.

LORD.[2] We'll show thee Io as she was a maid,
And how she was beguiled and surprised,
As lively painted as the deed was done.

THIRD SERVANT.[2] Or Daphne roaming through a thorny wood,
Scratching her legs that one shall swear she bleeds,
And at that sight shall sad Apollo weep,
So workmanly the blood and tears are drawn.

LORD.[3] Thou art a lord and nothing but a lord:
Thou hast a lady far more beautiful
Than any woman in this waning age.

FIRST SERVANT. And till the tears that she hath shed for thee
Like envious floods o'er-run her lovely face,
She was the fairest creature in the world;
And yet she is inferior to none.

SLY. Am I a lord,[4] and have I such a lady?[4]
Or do I dream?[5] or have I dream'd till now?[4]
I do not sleep:[5] I see, I hear, I speak;[4]
I smell sweet savour and I feel soft things:
Upon my life, I am a lord indeed
And not a tinker nor Christophero Sly.
Well, bring our lady hither to our sight;[6]
And once again, a pot o' the smallest ale.

SECOND SERVANT.[7] Will't please your mightiness to wash your hands?
O, how we joy to see your wit restored![8]
O, that once more you knew but what you are![8]
These fifteen years you have been in a dream;[8]
Or when you waked, so waked as if you slept.[8]

SLY. These fifteen years! by my fay, a goodly nap.
But did I never speak of all that time?

FIRST SERVANT.[9] O, yes, my lord, but very idle words:
For though you lay here in this goodly chamber,
Yet would you say ye were beaten out of door;
And rail upon the hostess of the house;
And say you would present her at the leet,
Because she brought stone jugs and no seal'd quarts:
Sometimes you would call out for Cicely Hacket.

SLY.[10] Ay, the woman's maid of the house.

THIRD SERVANT. Why, sir, you know no house nor no such maid,
Nor no such men as you have reckon'd up,
As Stephen Sly and old John Naps of Greece
And Peter Turph and Henry Pimpernell

[1] *Advancing.*

[2] *During these speeches* SLY *shows comic wonderment and appreciation.*

[3] SLY *shows great appreciation.*

[4] SERVANTS *bow " Yes."*

[5] SERVANTS *shake heads " No."*

[6] *Behaving as a Master giving orders.*

[7] *Advancing with bowl.*

[8] SLY *splashes* SERVANT.

[9] *Handing napkin.*

[10] *Returning napkin.*

And twenty more such names and men as these
Which never were nor no man ever saw.
    SLY.   Now Lord be thanked for my good amends !
    ALL.[1]   Amen.
    SLY.   I thank thee : thou shalt not lose by it.

PAGE *impersonating wife, who has been enjoying scene, advances.
    As he does so* SERVANTS *retire a little apart from bed.*

    PAGE.   How fares my noble lord ?
    SLY.   Marry, I fare well ; for here is cheer enough.
Where is my wife ?
    PAGE.   Here, noble lord : what is thy will with her ?
    SLY.[2]   Are you my wife and will not call me husband ?
My men should call me *lord* : I am your goodman.
    PAGE.[3]   My husband and my lord, my lord and husband ;
I am your wife in all obedience.
    SLY.   I know it well.   What must I call her ?
    LORD.   Madam.
    SLY.   Al'ce madam, or Joan madam ?
    LORD.   *Madam*, and nothing else : so lords call ladies.
    SLY.   Madam wife, they say that I have dream'd
And slept above some fifteen year or more.
    PAGE.   Ay, and the time seems thirty unto me,
Being all this time abandon'd from your bed.
    SLY.   'Tis much.   Servants, leave me and her alone.
Madam, undress you and come now to bed.
    PAGE.   Thrice-noble lord, let me entreat of you
To pardon me yet for a night or two,
Or, if not so, until the sun be set :
For your physicians have expressly charged,
In peril to incur your former malady,
That I should yet absent me from your bed :
I hope this reason stands for my excuse.
    SLY.   I would be loath to fall into my dreams again : I will therefore
tarry in despite of the flesh and blood.

Enter a MESSENGER C.

    LORD.   Your honour's players, hearing your amendment,
Are come to play a pleasant comedy ;
For so your doctors hold it very meet,
Seeing too much sadness hath congeal'd your blood,
And melancholy is the nurse of frenzy :
Therefore they thought it good you hear a play
And frame your mind to mirth and merriment,
Which bars a thousand harms and lengthens life.
    SLY.   Marry, I will, let them play it.[4]   Is not a comonty a Christmas
gambold or a tumbling-trick ?
    PAGE.   No, my good lord ; it is more pleasing stuff.
    SLY.   What, household stuff ?
    PAGE.   It is a kind of history.
    SLY.   Well, we'll see't.[5]   Come, madam wife, sit by my side and
let the world slip : we shall ne'er be younger.

              [*Musicians flourish for state business.*

Marginal notes (left column):

[1] *Fervently.*

[2] LORD *crosses at back of stage to* R. *of bed.*

[3] *Kneeling* L. *side of bed.*

[4] LORD *dismisses messenger to summon the players.*

[5] *Getting out of bed and sitting on the side.* FIRST SERVANT *puts slippers on* SLY. THIRD SERVANT *advances with rich gown. Amusing business as* SLY *gets into it. During this business* PAGE (*wife*) *retires to* L.C. *When* SLY *is dressed he struts down stage, extends his hand in great dignity to* PAGE *as he says, " Come, Madam Wife." The* SERVANTS, *walking backwards, precede him, bowing low in mock state and usher him to seat on balcony* L. *All form group about him.* PAGES, *carrying goblets and jugs stand on either side at his back.* LORD *follows and takes position near him. If there is no balcony* ᷍all *group on stage. As this business is being performed, attendants carry off bed* L.U.E. *Players' Tucket sounded off stage. The Players enter from the* R. *at* C. *Each advances, bows to* LORD *and* SLY (*who returns bow*) *and retires in turn up stage. The curtains (traverse 2) are drawn in front of them. Players Boy enters* R., *and exhibits Location Card " Before Baptista's House." He exhibits it to* SLY *and party, but at such an angle that the audience in the theatre see it. He bows to* SLY, *etc., and retires* R. *same entrance. Proscenium entrance.*

SCENE III

The Play.

Padua.   Before BAPTISTA'S *House.*

Enter LUCENTIO *and his man* TRANIO L.[1]

LUCENTIO.   Tranio, since for the great desire I had
To see fair Padua, nursery of arts,
I am arrived for fruitful Lombardy,
The pleasant garden of great Italy ;
And by my father's love and leave am arm'd
With his good will and thy good company,
My trusty servant, well approved in all,
Here let us breathe and haply institute
A course of learning and ingenious studies.[2]
Pisa renown'd for grave citizens
Gave me my being and my father first,
A merchant of great traffic through the world,
Vincentio, come of the Bentivolii.
Vincentio's son brought up in Florence
It shall become to serve all hopes conceived,
To deck his fortune with his virtuous deeds :[3]
And therefore, Tranio, for the time I study,
Virtue and that part of philosophy
Will I apply that treats of happiness
By virtue specially to be achieved.
Tell me thy mind ; for I have Pisa left
And am to Padua come, as he that leaves
A shallow plash to plunge him in the deep.[4]
And with satiety seeks to quench his thirst.

TRANIO.   *Mi perdonato,* gentle master mine,
I am in all affected as yourself ;
Glad that you thus continue your resolve
To suck the sweets of sweet philosophy.
Only, good master, while we do admire
This virtue and this moral discipline,
Let's be no stoics nor no stocks, I pray ;
Or so devote to Aristotle's checks
As Ovid be an outcast quite abjured :
Balk logic with acquaintance that you have
And practise rhetoric in your common talk ;
Music and poesy use to quicken you ;
The mathematics and the metaphysics,
Fall to them as you find your stomach serves you ;
No profit grows where is no pleasure ta'en :
In brief, sir, study what you most affect.

LUCENTIO.   Gramercies, Tranio, well dost thou advise.
If, Biondello, thou wert come ashore,
We could at once put us in readiness,
And take a lodging fit to entertain
Such friends as time in Padua shall beget.
But stay a while : what company is this ?

TRANIO.   Master, some show to welcome us to town.[5]

Enter BAPTISTA, KATHARINA, BIANCA, GREMIO, *and* HORTENSIO.[6]

LUCENTIO *and* TRANIO *stand aside* R.

BAPTISTA.   Gentlemen, importune me no farther,
For how I firmly am resolved you know ;

B

---

[1] *They bow to* LORD *and* SLY. SLY *applauds.*

[2] *Crossing the stage and addressing* SLY.

[3] *Back to* L. *of* TRANIO.

[4] *Crossing* R.

[5] *Crossing to corner* R.

[6] BAPTISTA *enters, coming to* C. *of stage speaking as he enters.* HORTENSIO *and* GREMIO *get between him and door* R. HORTENSIO *up stage,* GREMIO *below him.* KATHARINA *up stage* L. BIANCA *on* BAPTISTA'S L. *down stage.*

That is, not to bestow my youngest daughter
Before I have a husband for the elder:
If either of you both love Katharina,
Because I know you well and love you well,
Leave shall you have to court her at your pleasure.

GREMIO (*aside*).   To cart her rather: she's too rough for me.
There, there, Hortensio, will you any wife?

Moving down stage to BAPTISTA'S R.

KATHARINA.[1]   I pray you, sir, is it your will
To make a stale of me amongst these mates?

HORTENSIO.   Mates, maid! how mean you that? no mates for you,
Unless you were of gentler, milder mould.

Looking and jibing at BIANCA, *who moves in front of* BAPTISTA *to his* R. *hand.* KATHARINA *follows her to between* BAPTISTA *and* HORTENSIO *speaking to* HORTENSIO. *Then turns up stage behind* BAPTISTA *and getting to* L. *paces up and down stage between* SLY'S *group and the back.*

KATHARINA.[2]   I' faith, sir, you shall never need to fear:
I wis it is not half way to her heart;
But if it were, doubt not her care should be
To comb your noddle with a three-legg'd stool
And paint your face and use you like a fool.

HORTENSIO.   From all such devils, good Lord deliver us!

GREMIO.   And me too, good Lord!

TRANIO.   Hush, master! here's some good pastime toward:
That wench is stark mad or wonderful froward.

LUCENTIO.   But in the other's silence do I see
Maid's mild behaviour and sobriety.
Peace, Tranio!

TRANIO.   Well said, master; mum! and gaze your fill.

BAPTISTA.   Gentlemen, that I may soon make good
What I have said, Bianca, get you in:
And let it not displease thee, good Bianca,
For I will love thee ne'er the less, my girl.

Down stage L.

KATHARINA.[3]   A pretty peat! it is best
Put finger in the eye, an she knew why.

BIANCA.   Sister, content you in my discontent.
Sir, to your pleasure humbly I subscribe:
My books and instruments shall be my company,
On them to look and practise by myself.[4]

Going R. *to door sees* LUCENTIO, *stops* R., *looking demurely.*

LUCENTIO.   Hark, Tranio! thou may'st hear Minerva speak.

HORTENSIO.   Signor Baptista, will you be so strange?
Sorry am I that our good will effects
Bianca's grief.

GREMIO.   Why will you mew her up,
Signior Baptista, for this fiend of hell,
And make her bear the penance of her tongue?

Sees BIANCA *has not gone in.*
BIANCA exits hurriedly.

BAPTISTA.   Gentlemen, content ye; I am resolved:[5]
Go in, Bianca:[6]   [*Exit* BIANCA.
And for I know she taketh most delight
In music, instruments and poetry,
Schoolmasters will I keep within my house,
Fit to instruct her youth. If you, Hortensio,
Or Signior Gremio, you, know any such,
Prefer them hither; for to cunning men
I will be very kind, and liberal
To mine own children in good bringing up:
And so farewell. Katharina, you may stay;
For I have more to commune with Bianca.[7]   [*Exit.*

BAPTISTA bows to HORTENSIO *and* GREMIO, *and advances to door* R. *As he does so* HORTENSIO *and* GREMIO, *who are above him on his* R. *hand, bow to him stepping a little backwards and getting down stage in a line with door, their backs to* KATHARINA.
KATHARINA startles HORTENSIO *and* GREMIO *who jump back* UP *stage.*

KATHARINA.   Why, and I trust I may go too, may I not? What,
shall I be appointed hours; as though, belike, I knew not what to
take, and what to leave, ha?[8]   [*Exit.*

GREMIO.   You may go to the devil's dam: your gifts are so good, here's none will hold you.   Their love is not so great, Hortensio, but we may blow our nails together, and fast it fairly out: our cake's dough on both sides.[1] Farewell: yet, for the love I bear my sweet Bianca, if I can by any means light on a fit man to teach her that wherein she delights, I will wish him to her father.

HORTENSIO. So will I, Signior Gremio:[2] but a word, I pray. Though the nature of our quarrel yet never brooked parle, know now, upon advice, it toucheth us both, that we may yet again have access to our fair mistress and be happy rivals in Bianca's love, to labour and effect one thing specially.

GREMIO. What's that, I pray?

HORTENSIO. Marry, sir, to get a husband for her sister.

GREMIO. A husband! a devil.

HORTENSIO. I say, a husband.

GREMIO. I say, a devil.[3] Thinkest thou, Hortensio, though her father be very rich, any man is so very a fool to be married to hell?

HORTENSIO. Tush, Gremio, though it pass your patience and mine to endure her loud alarms, why, man, there be good fellows in the world, an a man could light on them, would take her with all faults, and money enough.

GREMIO. I cannot tell; but I had as lief take her dowry with this condition, to be whipped at the high cross every morning.

HORTENSIO. Faith, as you say, there's small choice in rotten apples. But come; since this bar in law makes us friends, it shall be so far forth friendly maintained till by helping Baptista's eldest daughter to a husband we set his youngest free for a husband and then have to 't afresh. Sweet Bianca! Happy man be his dole! He that runs fastest gets the ring. How say you, Signior Gremio?

GREMIO. I am agreed; and would I had given him the best horse in Padua to begin his wooing that would thoroughly woo her, wed her and bed her and rid the house of her! come on.

                    [Exit GREMIO and HORTENSIO L.

TRANIO.[4] I pray, sir, tell me, is it possible
That love should of a sudden take such hold?

LUCENTIO. O Tranio, till I found it to be true,
I never thought it possible or likely;
But see, while idly I stood looking on,
I found the effect of love in idleness:
And now in plainness do confess to thee,
That art to me as secret and as dear
As Anna to the queen of Carthage was,
Tranio, I burn, I pine, I perish, Tranio,
If I achieve not this young modest girl.
Counsel me, Tranio, for I know thou canst;
Assist me, Tranio, for I know thou wilt.

TRANIO. Master, it is no time to chide you now;
Affection is not rated from the heart:
If love have touch'd you, nought remains but so,
Redime te captum quam queas minimo.

LUCENTIO. Gramercies, lad, go forward; this contents?
The rest will comfort; for thy counsel's sound.

TRANIO. Master, you look'd so longly on the maid,
Perhaps you mark'd not what's the pith of all.

LUCENTIO. O yes, I saw sweet beauty in her face,
Such as the daughter of Agenor had,
That made great Jove to humble him to her hand,
When with his knees he kiss'd the Cretan strand.

TRANIO. Saw you no more? mark'd you not how her sister
Began to scold and raise up such a storm
That mortal ears might hardly endure the din?
    LUCENTIO. Tranio, I saw her coral lips to move
And with her breath she did perfume the air:
Sacred and sweet was all I saw in her.
    TRANIO. Nay, then, 'tis time to stir him from his trance,
I pray, awake, sir: if you love the maid,
Bend thoughts and wits to achieve her. Thus it stands:
Her eldest sister is so curst and shrewd
That till the father rid his hands of her,
Master, your love must live a maid at home;
And therefore has he closely mew'd her up,
Because she will not be annoy'd with suitors.

Crossing to R. of TRANIO, *looking towards door.*
Turning hopefully to TRANIO.

    LUCENTIO.[1] Ah, Tranio, what a cruel father's he![2]
But art thou not advised, he took some care
To get her cunning schoolmasters to instruct her?
    TRANIO. Ay, marry, am I, sir; and now 'tis plotted.
    LUCENTIO. I have it, Tranio.

Putting out hand.

    TRANIO.[3]   Master, for my hand,
Both our inventions meet and jump in one.
    LUCENTIO. Tell me thine first.
    TRANIO.   You will be schoolmaster
And undertake the teaching of the maid:
That's your device.

Taking hand.
Throwing hand away.

    LUCENTIO.   It is:[4] may it be done?
    TRANIO.[5] Not possible for who shall bear your part,
And be in Padua here Vincentio's son,
Keep house and ply his book, welcome his friends,
Visit his countrymen and banquet them?
    LUCENTIO. Basta; content thee, for I have it full.
We have not yet been seen in any house,
Nor can we be distinguish'd by our faces
For man or master; then it follows thus;
Thou shalt be master, Tranio, in my stead,
Keep house and port and servants, as I should:
I will some other be, some Florentine,
Some Neapolitan, or meaner man of Pisa.
'Tis hatch'd and shall be so: Tranio, at once

Changing hats and cloaks.

Uncase thee; take my colour'd hat and cloak:[6]
When Biondello comes, he waits on thee;
But I will charm him first to keep his tongue.
    TRANIO. So had you need.
In brief, sir, sith it your pleasure is,
And I am tied to be obedient;
For so your father charged me at our parting,
Be serviceable to my son, quoth he,
Although I think 'twas in another sense;
I am content to be Lucentio,

TRANIO L. LUCENTIO R.

Because so well I love Lucentio.[7]
    LUCENTIO. Tranio, be so, because Lucentio loves:
And let me be a slave, to achieve that maid
Whose sudden sight hath thrall'd my wounded eye.

LUCENTIO motions TRANIO R. *and crosses down L.*

Here comes the rogue.[8]

Enter BIONDELLO L. *with a bundle over his shoulder when* C. LUCENTIO
speaks.
    Sirrah, where have you been?

BIONDELLO.[1] Where have I been ! Nay, how now ! where are *you* ? Master, has my fellow Tranio stolen your clothes ? Or you stolen his ? or both ? pray, what's the news ?

LUCENTIO. Sirrah, come hither : 'tis no time to jest,
And therefore frame your manners to the time.
Your fellow Tranio here, to save my life,
Puts my apparel and my countenance on,
And I for my escape have put on his ;[2]
For in a quarrel since I came ashore
I kill'd a man and fear I was descried :[3]
Wait you on him, I charge you, as becomes,
While I make way from hence to save my life :
You understand me ?

BIONDELLO.   I, sir ! ne'er a whit.[4]

LUCENTIO. And not a jot of Tranio in your mouth :
Tranio is changed into Lucentio.

BIONDELLO. The better for him : would I were so too !

TRANIO. So could I, faith, boy, to have the next wish after,
That Lucentio indeed had Baptista's youngest daughter.
But, sirrah, not for my sake, but your master's, I advise
You use your manners discreetly in all kind of companies :
When I am alone, why, then I am Tranio ;
But in all places else your master Lucentio.

LUCENTIO. Tranio, let's go :[5] one thing more rests, that thyself execute, to make one among these wooers : if thou ask me why, sufficeth, my reasons are both good and weighty.

[*Exeunt* TRANIO *and* LUCENTIO *together, followed by* BIONDELLO R. *above door piece.*

As the players exeunt, the presenters forming the audience speak.

FIRST SERVANT. *My lord, you nod ; you do not mind the play.*

SLY. *Yes, by Saint Anne, do I. A good matter, surely : comes there any more of it ?*

PAGE. *My lord, 'tis but begun.*

SLY. *'Tis a very excellent piece of work, madam lady ; would 'twere done !*

[*They sit and mark.*

SCENE IV [6]

Padua. Before HORTENSIO'S *house.*

Enter L. PETRUCHIO *and his man* GRUMIO.[7]

PETRUCHIO. Verona, for a while I take my leave,
To see my friends in Padua, but of all
My best beloved and approved friend,
Hortensio ;[8] and I trow this is his house.[9]
Here, sirrah Grumio ; knock, I say.

GRUMIO. Knock, sir ! whom should I knock ? is there any man has rebused your worship ?

PETRUCHIO. Villain, I say, knock me here soundly.

GRUMIO. Knock you here, sir ! why, sir, what am I, sir, that I should knock you here, sir ?

PETRUCHIO. Villain, I say, knock me at this gate
And rap me well, or I'll knock your knave's pate.

[1] BIONDELLO *looks puzzled, first at the one, then at the other.*

[2] BIONDELLO *drops bundle.*

[3] BIONDELLO *sits on bundle.*

[4] *Looking at* TRANIO.

[5] LUCENTIO *goes* R. *above* BIONDELLO, TRANIO *joins him.*

[6] *Enter Players' boy from* R. *proscenium entrance. He exhibits location card " Before Hortensio's house " with business as before. He retires same entrance.*

[7] *They enter from space between Traverse No. 2 and door piece.* PETRUCHIO *comes down stage* C. ; GRUMIO *above him* L.C. *They bow to* SLY.

[8] *As he speaks he gets to* R., *turns.*
[9] *Indicating house* L.

GRUMIO. My master is grown quarrelsome. I should knock you first,
And then I know after who comes by the worst.
PETRUCHIO. Will it not be ?
Faith, sirrah, an you'll not knock, I'll ring it ;
I'll try how you can sol, fa, and sing it.

[*He wrings him by the ears.*[1]

GRUMIO. Help, masters, help ! my master is mad.
PETRUCHIO. Now, knock when I bid you, sirrah villain !

Enter HORTENSIO. *From door* L.

HORTENSIO. How now ! what's the matter ? My old friend Grumio ! and my good friend Petruchio ! How do you all at Verona ?[2]
PETRUCHIO. Signior Hortensio, come you to part the fray ?
Con tutto il cuore, ben trovato, may I say.
HORTENSIO. *Alla nostra casa ben venuto, molto honorato signor mio Petruchio.*
Rise, Grumio, rise :[3] we will compound this quarrel.
GRUMIO. Nay, 'tis no matter, sir, what he 'leges in Latin. If this be not a lawful cause for me to leave his service, look you, sir, he bid me knock him and rap him soundly, sir : well, was it fit for a servant to use his master so, being perhaps, for aught I see, two and thirty, a pip out ?
Whom would to God I had well knock'd at first,
Then had not Grumio come by the worst.
PETRUCHIO. A senseless villain ! Good Hortensio,
I bade the rascal knock upon your gate
And could not get him for my heart to do it.
GRUMIO. Knock at the gate ! O heavens ! Spake you not these words plain, *Sirrah, knock me here, rap me here, knock me well, and knock me soundly ?* And come you now with, *knocking at the gate ?*
PETRUCHIO. Sirrah, be gone, or talk not, I advise you.[4]
HORTENSIO. Petruchio, patience ; I am Grumio's pledge :
Why, this's a heavy chance 'twixt him and you,
Your ancient, trusty, pleasant servant Grumio.
And tell me now, sweet friend, what happy gale
Blows you to Padua here from old Verona ?
PETRUCHIO. Such wind as scatters young men through the world
To seek their fortunes farther than at home
Where small experience grows. But in a few,
Signior Hortensio, thus it stands with me :
Antonio, my father, is deceased ;
And I have thrust myself into this maze,
Haply to wive and thrive as best I may :
Crowns in my purse I have and goods at home,
And so am come abroad to see the world.
HORTENSIO. Petruchio, shall I then come roundly to thee
And wish thee to a shrewd ill-favour'd wife ?
Thou 'ldst thank me but a little for my counsel :
And yet I'll promise thee she shall be rich
And very rich : but thou'rt too much my friend,
And I'll not wish thee to her.[5]
PETRUCHIO. Signior Hortensio, 'twixt such friends as we
Few words suffice ; and therefore, if thou know
One rich enough to be Petruchio's wife,
As wealth is burden of my wooing dance,

[1] *Both* R.O. GRUMIO *on his knees.*

[2] PETRUCHIO *crossing in front of* GRUMIO.

[3] *Crossing* PETRUCHIO *to* O. GRUMIO *rises and gets* R. PETRUCHIO L.

[4] PETRUCHIO *advances towards* GRUMIO R. *in front of* HORTENSIO. GRUMIO *gets across behind* HORTENSIO *to* L.C. *up stage.* PETRUCHIO *stays on* HORTENSIO'S R. *hand.*

[5] HORTENSIO *turns away from* PETRUCHIO, *getting* L.C. *down stage—stops and faces* PETRUCHIO, *who advances as he speaks to* R.O. *down stage.*

Be she as foul as was Florentius' love,
As old as Sibyl and as curst and shrewd
As Socrates' Xanthippe, or a worse,
She moves me not, or not removes, at least,
Affection's edge in me, were she as rough
As are the swelling Adriatic seas :
I come to wive it wealthily in Padua ;
If wealthily, then happily in Padua.[1]

GRUMIO.[2] Nay, look you, sir, he tells you flatly what his mind is :
why, give him gold enough and marry him to a puppet or an aglet-
baby ; or an old trot with ne'er a tooth in her head, though she have
as many diseases as two and fifty horses : why, nothing comes amiss,
so money comes withal.

HORTENSIO.[3] Petruchio, since we are stepp'd thus far in,
I will continue that I broach'd in jest.
I can, Petruchio, help thee to a wife
With wealth enough and young and beauteous,
Brought up as best becomes a gentlewoman :
Her only fault, and that is faults enough,
Is that she is intolerable curst
And shrewd and froward, so beyond all measure
That, were my state far worser than it is,
I would not wed her for a mine of gold.

PETRUCHIO. Hortensio, peace ! thou know'st not gold's effect :
Tell me her father's name and 'tis enough ;
For I will board her, though she chide as loud
As thunder when the clouds in autumn crack.

HORTENSIO. Her father is Baptista Minola,
An affable and courteous gentleman :
Her name is Katharina Minola,
Renown'd in Padua for her scolding tongue.

PETRUCHIO. I know her father, though I know not her ;
And he knew my deceased father well.
I will not sleep, Hortensio, till I see her ;[4]
And therefore let me be thus bold with you
To give you over at this first encounter,
Unless you will accompany me thither.

GRUMIO.[5] I pray you, sir, let him go while the humour lasts. O'
my word, an she knew him as well as I do, she would think scolding
would do little good upon him : she may perhaps call him half a score
knaves or so : why, that's nothing ; an he begin once, he'll rail in
his rope-tricks. I'll tell you what, sir, an she stand him but a little,
he will throw a figure in her face and so disfigure her with it that she
shall have no more eyes to see withal than a cat. You know him not,
sir.

HORTENSIO.[6] Tarry, Petruchio, I must go with thee,
For in Baptista's keep my treasure is :
He hath the jewel of my life in hold,
His youngest daughter, beautiful Bianca,
And her withholds from me and other more,
Suitors to her and rivals in my love,
Supposing it a thing impossible,
For those defects I have before rehearsed,
That ever Katharina will be woo'd ;
Therefore this order hath Baptista ta'en,
That none shall have access unto Bianca
Till Katharine the curst have got a husband.

[1] PETRUCHIO *gets* R.

[2] *Coming down stage to* HORTENSIO'S *left hand.*

[3] *Going to* PETRUCHIO *amused at* GRUMIO'S *speech.*

[4] *Crosses stage* L., *turns to face* HORTENSIO *as he concludes speech.* HORTENSIO *makes gesture to detain him.*

[5] GRUMIO *crosses in front of* PETRUCHIO *as he addresses* HORTENSIO.

[6] *Advancing in front of* GRUMIO *to* PETRU-CHIO.

GRUMIO. Katharine the curst!
A title for a maid of all titles the worst.
   HORTENSIO. Now shall my friend Petruchio do me grace,
And offer me disguised in sober robes
To old Baptista as a schoolmaster
Well seen in music, to instruct Bianca;
That so I may, by this device, at least
Have leave and leisure to make love to her
And unsuspected court her by herself.
   GRUMIO. Here's no knavery! See, to beguile the old folks how
the young folks lay their heads together!

Enter GREMIO, *and* LUCENTIO *disguised* L.

Master, master, look about you: who goes there, ha? [1]
   HORTENSIO. Peace, Grumio! it is the rival of my love.
Petruchio, stand by a while.
   GRUMIO. A proper stripling and an amorous! [2]
   GREMIO. O, very well; I have perused the note.
Hark you, sir; I'll have them very fairly bound:
All books of love, see that at any hand;
And see you read no other lectures to her:
You understand me: over and beside
Signior Baptista's liberality,
I'll mend it with a largess. Take your papers too.
And let me have them very well perfumed:
For she is sweeter than perfume itself
To whom they go to. What will you read to her?
   LUCENTIO. Whate'er I read to her, I'll plead for you
As for my patron, stand you so assured,
As firmly as yourself were still in place:
Yea, and perhaps with more successful words
Than you, unless you were a scholar, sir.
   GREMIO. O this learning, what a thing it is!
   GRUMIO. O this woodcock, what an ass it is!
   PETRUCHIO. Peace, sirrah!
   HORTENSIO. Grumio, mum! God save you, Signior Gremio. [2]
   GREMIO. And you are well met, Signior Hortensio.
Trow you whither I am going? To Baptista Minola.
I promised to inquire carefully
About a schoolmaster for the fair Bianca:
And by good fortune I have lighted well
On this young man, for learning and behaviour
Fit for her turn, well read in poetry,
And other books, good ones, I warrant ye.
   HORTENSIO. [4] 'Tis well; and I have met a gentleman
Hath promised me to help me to another,
A fine musician to instruct our mistress
So shall I no whit be behind in duty
To fair Bianca, so beloved of me.
   GREMIO. Beloved of me; and that my deeds shall prove.
   GRUMIO. And that his bags shall prove.
   HORTENSIO. Gremio, 'tis now no time to vent our love;
Listen to me, and if you speak me fair
I'll tell you news indifferent good for either.
Here is a gentleman whom by chance I met,
Upon agreement from us to his liking,

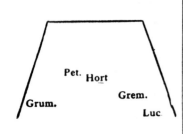

Pet. Hort
Grem.
Grum.   Luc.

Will undertake to woo curst Katharine,
Yea, and to marry her, if her dowry please.

GREMIO. So said, so done, is well.
Hortensio, have you told him all her faults ?

PETRUCHIO. I know she is an irksome brawling scold :
If that be all, masters, I hear no harm.

GREMIO. No, say'st me so, friend ? What countryman ?

PETRUCHIO.[1] Born in Verona, old Antonio's son :
My father dead, my fortune lives for me ;
And I do hope good days and long to see.

GREMIO. O sir, such a life, with such a wife, were strange !
But if you have a stomach, to 't i' God's name :
You shall have me assisting you in all.
But will you woo this wild-cat ?

PETRUCHIO.   Will I live ?

GREMIO. Will he woo her ? ay, or I'll hang her.

PETRUCHIO. Why came I hither but to that intent ?[2]
Think you a little din can daunt mine ears ?
Have I not in my time heard lions roar ?
Have I not heard the sea puff'd up with winds
Rage like an angry boar chafed with sweat ?
Have I not heard great ordnance in the field,
And heaven's artillery thunder in the skies ?
Have I not in a pitched battle heard
Loud 'larums, neighing steeds, and trumpets' clang ?
And do you tell me of a woman's tongue,
That gives not half so great a blow to hear
As will a chestnut in a farmer's fire ?
Tush, tush ! fear boys with bugs.[3]

GRUMIO.   For he fears none.

GREMIO.[4] Hortensio, hark :
This gentleman is happily arrived
My mind presumes, for his own good and ours.

HORTENSIO. I promised we would be contributors
And bear his charge of wooing, whatsoe'er.

GREMIO. And so we will, provided that he win her.

GRUMIO. I would I were as sure of a good dinner.

Enter TRANIO *bravely apparelled, and* BIONDELLO L.[5]

TRANIO. Gentlemen, God save you. If I may be bold,
Tell me, I beseech you, which is the readiest way
To the house of Signior Baptista Minola ?

GREMIO. He that has the two fair daughters : is't he you mean ?[6]

TRANIO. Even he.[7]

GREMIO. Hark you, sir ; you mean not her to—

TRANIO. Perhaps, him and her, sir : what have you to do ?

PETRUCHIO.[8] Not her that chides, sir, at any hand, I pray.

TRANIO. I love no chiders, sir. Biondello. let's away.

LUCENTIO. Well begun, Tranio.

HORTENSIO [9] Sir, a word ere you go ;
Are you a suitor to the maid you talk of, yea or no ?

TRANIO.[10] And if I be, sir, is it any offence ?

GREMIO. No ; if without more words you will get you hence.

TRANIO. Why, sir, I pray, are not the streets as free
For me as for you ?[11]

GREMIO.   But so is not she.

---

[1] *Crossing in front of* HORTENSIO *to* GREMIO. HORTENSIO *gets from* C. *to* R.C.

[2] GRUMIO *down* R. HORTENSIO R.C. PETRUCHIO C. GREMIO *on* PETRUCHIO'S L. *and* LUCENTIO *down* L.

[3] PETRUCHIO *turns up stage at end of speech and gets round to* R.C. *up stage where* GRUMIO *joins him.*

[4] *Moves to* HORTENSIO.

[5] *As they enter,* GRUMIO *leaves* PETRUCHIO *and comes down stage extreme* R. *All face* TRANIO.

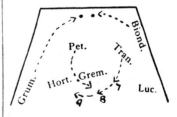

[10] GREMIO *crosses to* L.C. *down stage.*

[11] TRANIO *turning to* GREMIO *and coming to* C.

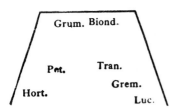

¹ *To* LUCENTIO.

² R. *of* HORTENSIO.

⁴ *Going to* TRANIO.

TRANIO. For what reason, I beseech you ?

GREMIO.   For this reason, if you'll know,
That she's the choice love of Signior Gremio.

1. ORTENSIO. That she's the chosen of Signior Hortensio.¹

TRANIO. Softly, my masters ! if you be gentlemen,
Do me this right ; hear me with patience.
Baptista is a noble gentleman,
To whom my father is not all unknown ;
And were his daughter fairer than she is,
She may more suitors have and me for one.
Fair Leda's daughter had a thousand wooers ;
Then well one more may fair Bianca have :
And so she shall ; Lucentio shall make one,
Though Paris came in hope to speed alone.

GREMIO. What ! this gentleman will out-talk us all.²

LUCENTIO. Sir, give him head : I know he'll prove a jade.

PETRUCHIO. Hortensio, to what end are all these words ?³

HORTENSIO. Let me be so bold as ask you,
Did you yet ever see Baptista's daughter ?

TRANIO. No, sir ; but hear I do that he hath two,
The one as famous for a scolding tongue
As is the other for beauteous modesty.

PETRUCHIO. Sir, sir, the first's for me ; let her go by.⁴

GREMIO. Yea, leave that labour to great Hercules ;
And let it be more than Alcides' twelve.

PETRUCHIO. Sir, understand you this of me in sooth :
The youngest daughter whom you hearken for
Her father keeps from all access of suitors,
And will not promise her to any man
Until the elder sister first be wed :
The younger then is free and not before.

TRANIO. If it be so, sir, that you are the man
Must stead us all and me amongst the rest,
And if you break the ice and do this feat,
Achieve the elder, set the younger free
For our access, whose hap shall be to have her
Will not so graceless be to be ingrate.

HORTENSIO. Sir, you say well and well you do conceive ;
And since you do profess to be a suitor,
You must, as we do, gratify this gentleman,
To whom we all rest generally beholding.

TRANIO. Sir, I shall not be slack : in sign whereof,
Please ye we may contrive this afternoon,
And quaff carouses to our mistress' health,
And do as adversaries do in law,
Strive mightily, but eat and drink as friends.⁵

GRUMIO. *and* BIONDELLO. O excellent motion ! Fellows, let's
        be gone.

HORTENSIO. The motion's good indeed and be it so,
Petruchio, I shall be your *ben venuto.*

[*Exeunt* R.⁶

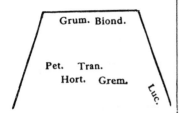

⁶ HORTENSIO *and* PERTUCHIO *together*
followed by TRANIO. GREMIO *and* LUCEN-
TIO *togeth.? followed by* GRUMIO *and*
BIONDELLO.
As they go. Traverse No. 2 is drawn off
exposing full set.

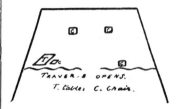

SCENE V

Padua. BAPTISTA'S *house.*

Enter KATHARINA *and* BIANCA, C.[1]

BIANCA. Good sister, wrong me not, nor wrong yourself,
To make a bondmaid and a slave of me ;
That I disdain : but for these other gawds,
Unbind my hands, I'll pull them off myself,
Yea, all my raiment, to my petticoat ;
Or what you will command me will I do,
So well I know my duty to my elders.[2]
    KATHARINA. Of all thy suitors, here I charge thee, tell
Whom thou lovest best : see thou dissemble not.
    BIANCA.[3] Believe me, sister, of all the men alive
I never yet beheld that special face
Which I could fancy more than any other.
    KATHARINA. Minion, thou liest. Is't not Hortensio ?
    BIANCA. If you affect him, sister, here I swear
I'll plead for you myself, but you shall have him.
    KATHARINA. O then, belike, you fancy riches more :
You will have Gremio to keep you fair.
    BIANCA. Is it for him you do envy me so ?
Nay then you jest, and now I well perceive
You have but jested with me all this while :
I prithee, sister Kate, untie my hands.
    KATHARINA. If that be jest, then all the rest was so.
                                    [Strikes her.

Enter BAPTISTA, C.

BAPTISTA. Why, how now, dame ! whence grows this insolence ?
Bianca, stand aside. Poor girl ! she weeps.
Go ply thy needle ; meddle not with her.
For shame, thou hilding of a devilish spirit,
Why dost thou wrong her that did ne'er wrong thee ?
When did she cross thee with a bitter word ?
    KATHARINA.[5] Her silence flouts me, and I'll be revenged.[6]
    BAPTISTA. What, in my sight ? Bianca, get thee in.[7]
                              [Exit BIANCA.
    KATHARINA.[8] What, will you not suffer me ? Nay, now I see
She is your treasure, she must have a husband ;
I must dance bare-foot on her wedding day
And for your love to her lead apes in hell.[9]
Talk not to me : I will go sit and weep
Till I can find occasion of revenge.   *[Exit* C.
    BAPTISTA.[10] Was ever gentleman thus grieved as I ?
But who comes here ?

Enter GREMIO, LUCENTIO *in the habit of a mean man ;* PETRUCHIO,
with HORTENSIO *as a musician ; and* TRANIO, *with* BIONDELLO
bearing a lute and books.[11]

GREMIO.[12] Good morrow, neighbour Baptista.

[1] KATHARINA *walks round stage followed by*
BIANCA.

[2] KATHARINA L., BIANCA C.

[3] BIANCA *on knees.*

[4] KATHARINA *falls back* L.

[5] *Advancing to* BAPTISTA.
[6] BIANCA *gets behind* BAPTISTA.
[7] BAPTISTA *takes* BIANCA *up stage. She
exits* C.

[8] *Advancing on* BAPTISTA. *who comes down
R.C. by chair at table.*

[9] BAPTISTA *makes an imperious gesture.*

[10] *Falls into chair* R.

[11] *At centre entrance.*
            1. GREMIO.
            2. LUCENTIO.
Order of entrance 3. PETRUCHIO.
            4. HORTENSIO.
            5. TRANIO.
            6. BIONDELLO.
[12] *Down to* BAPTISTA.

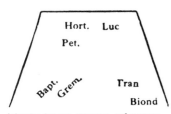

[1] *Coming between* BAPTISTA *and* GREMIO.

HORTENSIO *advances down stage* C.

[3] PETRUCHIO *turns sharply up stage as though to exit* C. *Is stayed by* HORTENSIO. LUCENTIO, TRANIO, GREMIO *move to stay him.*

[4] *Coming back to* BAPTISTA *as others fall into former positions.*

[5] *Shaking hands heartily.*

[7] *Moving round to* L. *of* GREMIO, *then to back of table* R.
[8] *Motions* LUCENTIO *forward.*

[9] *Passes* GREMIO *over to* R.
[10] LUCENTIO *bows and retires to chair* L.

[11] *Coming forward.*

[12] *Hands* BAPTISTA *a letter.*

BAPTISTA.[1] Good morrow, neighbour Gremio. God save you. gentlemen !

PETRUCHIO.[2] And you, good sir ! Pray, have you not a daughter Call'd Katharina, fair and virtuous ?

BAPTISTA. I have a daughter, sir, called Katharina.

GREMIO. You are too blunt : go to it orderly.

PETRUCHIO. You wrong me, Signior Gremio : give me leave.
I am a gentleman of Verona, sir,
That, hearing of her beauty and her wit,
Her affability and bashful modesty,
Her wondrous qualities and mild behaviour,
Am bold to show myself a forward guest
Within your house, to make mine eye the witness
Of that report which I so oft have heard.
And, for an entrance to my entertainment,
I do present you with a man of mine,

[*Presenting* HORTENSIO.[3]

Cunning in music and the mathematics,
To instruct her fully in those sciences,
Whereof I know she is not ignorant :
Accept of him, or else you do me wrong :
His name is Licio, born in Mantua.

BAPTISTA. You're welcome, sir ; and he, for your good sake.
But for my daughter Katharine, this I know,
She is not for your turn, the more my grief.

PETRUCHIO. I see you do not mean to part with her,
Or else you like not of my company.[4]

BAPTISTA. Mistake me not ; I speak but as I find.
Whence are you, sir ? what may I call your name ?

PETRUCHIO.[5] Petruchio is my name ; Antonio's son,
A man well known throughout all Italy.

BAPTISTA. I know him well : you are welcome for his sake.[6]

GREMIO. Saving your tale, Petruchio, I pray,
Let us, that are poor petitioners, speak too :
Beccare ! you are marvellous forward.

PETRUCHIO. O, pardon me, Signior Gremio ; I would fain be doing.[7]

GREMIO. I doubt it not, sir ; but you will curse your wooing.[8]
Neighbour, this is a gift very grateful, I am sure of it. To express the like kindness, myself, that have been more kindly beholding to you than any, freely give unto you this young scholar [*presenting* LUCENTIO], that hath been long studying at Rheims ; as cunning in Greek, Latin, and other languages, as the other in music and mathematics : his name is Cambio ; pray, accept his service.

BAPTISTA. A thousand thanks, Signior Gremio.[9] Welcome, good Cambio.[10] [*To* TRANIO] But, gentle sir, methinks you walk like a stranger : may I be so bold to know the cause of your coming ?

TRANIO.[11] Pardon me, sir, the boldness is mine own,
That, being a stranger in this city here,
Do make myself a suitor to your daughter,
Unto Bianca, fair and virtuous.[12]
Nor is your firm resolve unknown to me,
In the preferment of the eldest sister.
This liberty is all that I request,
That, upon knowledge of my parentage,
I may have welcome 'mongst the rest that woo
And free access and favour as the rest :

And, toward the education of your daughters,
I here bestow a simple instrument,
And this small packet of Greek and Latin books :
If you accept them, then their worth is great.
    BAPTISTA.   Lucentio is your name ; of whence, I pray ?
    TRANIO.   Of Pisa, sir ; son to Vincentio.
    BAPTISTA.   A mighty man of Pisa ; by report
I know him well : you are very welcome, sir.
Take you the lute, and you the set of books ;
You shall go see your pupils presently.[1]
Holla, within ! [2]

Enter a SERVANT.[3]

          Sirrah, lead these gentlemen
To my daughters ; and tell them both,
These are their tutors : bid them use them well.

[*Exit* SERVANT, *with* LUCENTIO *and* HORTENSIO, BIONDELLO
following C.

We will go walk a little in the orchard,
And then to dinner.[4] You are passing welcome,
And so I pray you all to think yourselves.
    PETRUCHIO.[5]   Signior Baptista, my business asketh haste,
And every day I cannot come to woo.
You knew my father well, and in him me,
Left solely heir to all his lands and goods,
Which I have better'd rather than decreased :
Then tell me, if I get your daughter's love,
What dowry shall I have with her to wife ?
    BAPTISTA.   After my death the one half of my lands,
And in possession twenty thousand crowns.
    PETRUCHIO.   And, for that dowry, I'll assure her of
Her widowhood, be it that she survive me,
In all my lands and leases whatsoever :
Let specialties be therefore drawn between us,
That covenants may be kept on either hand.
    BAPTISTA.   Ay, when the special thing is well obtain'd,
That is, her love ; for that is all in all.
    PETRUCHIO.   Why, that is nothing ; for I tell you, father,
I am as peremptory as she proud-minded ;
And where two raging fires meet together
They do consume the thing that feeds their fury :
Though little fire grows great with little wind,
Yet extreme gusts will blow out fire and all :
So I to her and so she yields to me ;
For I am rough and woo not like a babe.
    BAPTISTA.   Well mayst thou woo, and happy be thy speed !
But be thou arm'd for some unhappy words.
    PETRUCHIO.   Ay, to the proof ; as mountains are for winds,
That shake not, though they blow perpetually.

Re-enter HORTENSIO, *with his head broken* C.

    BAPTISTA.   How now, my friend ! why dost thou look so pale ?
    HORTENSIO.[6]   For fear, I promise you, if I look pale.

[1] HORTENSIO *advances to* BIONDELLO *and takes lute.* LUCENTIO *takes books.*
[2] *Moving to* O. *up stage and returning.*

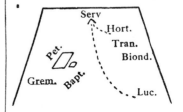

[4] *Moving up to* O.

[5] *Taking him by the arm, bringing him down stage.*

[6] *Sitting chair* L.

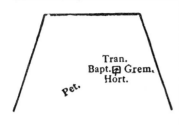

Tran.
Bapt. ⊕ Grem.
Hort.

Pet.

[1] *All look at* PETRUCHIO *as pointing out his fate.*

[2] *All regard* PETRUCHIO *with comic sympathy as they exit. Making actions to one another.*

[4] PETRUCHIO *crosses to* L. *down stage.*

[5] *As* KATHARINA *enters and sees* PETRUCHIO, *she glares at him from* C. *up stage, then coming down, turns from him to* R., *sweeping round up* R. *round table in great disdain and comes to* C. *confronting* PETRUCHIO *in anger.*

[6] PETRUCHIO *circles up* L. *behind* KATHARINA *somewhat in imitation of her action. He speaks over her right shoulder.* KATHARINA *looks away, tapping her boot on the floor.*

[7] *Suddenly facing him.*

[8] *Sweeping down stage* R. *below table.*

[9] *Moving round above table and facing* KATHARINA *extreme* R. KATHARINA *backs a little away to* R.C.

[10] PETRUCHIO *goes in front of* KATHARINA *and sits carelessly in chair* L.

[11] *Moving slowly and scornfully to* C.

BAPTISTA. What, will my daughter prove a good musician ?[1]
HORTENSIO. I think she'll sooner prove a soldier:
Iron may hold with her, but never lutes.
BAPTISTA. Why, then thou canst not break her to the lute ?
HORTENSIO. Why, no; for she hath broke the lute to me.
I did but tell her she mistook her frets,
And bow'd her hand to teach her fingering;
When, with a most impatient devilish spirit,
Frets, call you these ? quoth she; *I'll fume with them !*
And, with that word, she struck me on the head,
And through the instrument my pate made way;
And there I stood amazed for a while,
As on a pillory, looking through the lute;
While she did call me rascal fiddler
And twangling Jack; with twenty such vile terms,
As had she studied to misuse me so.[2]
PETRUCHIO. Now, by the world, it is a lusty wench;
I love her ten times more than e'er I did:
O, how I long to have some chat with her !
BAPTISTA. Well, go with me and be not so discomfited:
Proceed in practice with my younger daughter;
She's apt to learn and thankful for good turns.
Signior Petruchio, will you go with us,
Or shall I send my daughter Kate to you ?
PETRUCHIO. I pray you do. [*Exeunt all but* PETRUCHIO C.[3]
I will attend her here,
And woo her with some spirit when she comes.
Say that she rail; why then I'll tell her plain
She sings as sweetly as a nightingale:
Say that she frown; I'll say she looks as clear
As morning roses newly wash'd with dew:
Say she be mute and will not speak a word;
Then I'll commend her volubility,
And say she uttereth piercing eloquence:
If she do bid me pack, I'll give her thanks,
As though she bid me stay by her a week:
If she deny to wed, I'll crave the day
When I shall ask the banns and when be married.
But here she comes; and now, Petruchio, speak.[4]

Enter KATHARINA C.[5]

[6]Good morrow, Kate; for that's your name, I hear.
KATHARINA.[7] Well, have you heard, but something hard of hearing:
They call me Katharine that do talk of me.[8]
PETRUCHIO.[9] You lie, in faith; for you are call'd plain Kate,
And bonny Kate and sometimes Kate the curst;
But Kate, the prettiest Kate in Christendom,
Kate of Kate Hall, my super-dainty Kate,
For dainties are all Kates, and therefore, Kate,
Take this of me. Kate of my consolation;
Hearing thy mildness praised in every town,
Thy virtues spoke of, and thy beauty sounded,
Yet not so deeply as to thee belongs,
Myself am moved to woo thee for my wife.[10]
KATHARINA. Moved ! in good time: let him that moved you hither
Remove you hence: I knew you at the first
You were a moveable.[11]

PETRUCHIO.	Why, what's a moveable ?
KATHARINA.[1]	A join'd-stool.
PETRUCHIO.[2]	Thou hast hit it: come, sit on me.
KATHARINA.	Asses are made to bear, and so are you.
PETRUCHIO.	Women are made to bear, and so are you.
KATHARINA.	No such jade as you, if me you mean.

PETRUCHIO. Alas! good Kate, I will not burden thee ;
For, knowing thee to be but young and light—

KATHARINA. Too light for such a swain as you to catch ;
And yet as heavy as my weight should be.

PETRUCHIO. Should be ! should—buzz !

KATHARINA.   Well ta'en, and like a buzzard.

PETRUCHIO. O slow-wing'd turtle ! shall a buzzard take thee ?

KATHARINA. Ay, for a turtle, as he takes a buzzard.

PETRUCHIO. Come, come, you wasp ; i' faith, you are too angry.

KATHARINA. If I be waspish, best beware my sting.

PETRUCHIO. My remedy is then, to pluck it out.

KATHARINA. Ay, if the fool could find it where it lies.

PETRUCHIO. Who knows not where a wasp does wear his sting ?
   In his tail.

KATHARINA. In his tongue.

PETRUCHIO. Whose tongue ?

KATHARINA. Yours, if you talk of tails: and so farewell.[3]

PETRUCHIO. What, with my tongue in your tail ?[4] nay, come
   again,
Good Kate ; I am a gentleman.

KATHARINA.   That I'll try.[5]

PETRUCHIO.[6] I swear I'll cuff you, if you strike again.

KATHARINA. So may you lose your arms :
If you strike me, you are no gentleman ;
And if no gentleman, why then no arms.[7]

PETRUCHIO.[8] A herald, Kate ? O, put me in thy books !

KATHARINA. What is your crest ? a coxcomb ?

PETRUCHIO. A combless cock, so Kate will be my hen.

KATHARINA.[9] No cock of mine ; you crow too like a craven.

PETRUCHIO.[10] Nay, come, Kate, come ; you must not look so sour.

KATHARINA. It is my fashion, when I see a crab.

PETRUCHIO. Why, here's no crab ; and therefore look not sour.

KATHARINA. There is, there is.

PETRUCHIO. Then show it me.

KATHARINA. Had I a glass, I would.

PETRUCHIO. What, you mean my face ?

KATHARINA. Well aim'd of such a young one.

PETRUCHIO. Now, by Saint George, I am too young for you.

KATHARINA. Yet you are wither'd.

PETRUCHIO. 'Tis with cares.

KATHARINA. I care not.[11]

PETRUCHIO.[12] Nay, hear you, Kate: in sooth you scape not so.

KATHARINA. I chafe you, if I tarry : let me go.

PETRUCHIO. No, not a whit :[13] I find you passing gentle.
'Twas told me you were rough and coy and sullen,
And now I find report a very liar ;[14]
For thou art pleasant, gamesome, passing courteous,[15]
But slow in speech, yet sweet as spring-time flowers :
Thou canst not frown, thou canst not look askance,
Nor bite the lip, as angry wenches will,[16]
Nor hast thou pleasure to be cross in talk

[1] KATHARINA *moves one step to go up* C.

[2] PETRUCHIO *rises, reaching out with his right hand he catches* KATHARINE *by her left wrist as her back is turned to him, swings her completely round and across to chair until at the end of the swing she is facing him.* PETRUCHIO'S *position at this moment must be such as he can fall easily into chair.* KATHARINA *attacks his hold with her* R. *hand.* PETRUCHIO *secures both her wrists, pulling her on to his* R. *knee, as he sits and holds her fast.*

[3] KATHARINA *has wriggled herself to a standing position.* PETRUCHIO *has still both her hands.*
[4] *Pulling her again on to his knee.*

[5] *She strikes him and breaks away to* C.
[6] *Rising.*

[7] *Across front of* PETRUCHIO *to* L.
[8] PETRUCHIO *follows her.*

[9] *Across to* R.
[10] PETRUCHIO *follows again.*

[11] KATHARINA *turns with a flounce in front of* PETRUCHIO *and moves quickly up to* C. *exit.*
[12] PETRUCHIO *is quicker and gets in front of her, staying her.*
[13] KATHARINA *sweeps down* L. *fuming.*

[14] KATHARINA *returns to* PETRUCHIO, *demanding in action that he let her pass. She steps to* R. *and* L. *of* PETRUCHIO, *he intercepting her each time.*
[15] KATHARINA *gives up her efforts and returns down stage* R.

[16] KATHARINA *up to* PETRUCHIO *again, round table* R.

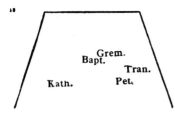

But thou with mildness entertain'st thy wooers,
With gentle conference, soft and affable.[1]
Why does the world report that Kate doth limp?[2]
O slanderous world! Kate like the hazel-twig
Is straight and slender and as brown in hue
As hazel nuts and sweeter than the kernels.[3]
O, let me see thee walk:[4] thou dost not halt.
    KATHARINA.[5] Go, fool, and whom thou keep'st command.
    PETRUCHIO. Did ever Dian so become a grove
As Kate this chamber with her princely gait?
O, be thou Dian, and let her be Kate;
And then let Kate be chaste and Dian sportful![6]
    KATHARINA. Where did you study all this goodly speech?
    PETRUCHIO. It is extempore, from my mother-wit.
    KATHARINA. A witty mother! witless else her son.
    PETRUCHIO. Am I not wise?
    KATHARINA. Yes; keep you warm.[7]
    PETRUCHIO.[8] Marry, so I mean, sweet Katharine, in thy bed;
And therefore, setting all this chat aside,
Thus in plain terms: your father hath consented
That you shall be my wife; your dowry 'greed on;
And, will you, nill you, I will marry you.
Now, Kate, I am a husband for your turn;
For, by this light, whereby I see thy beauty,
Thy beauty, that doth make me like thee well,
Thou must be married to no man but me;
For I am he am born to tame you Kate,
And bring you from a wild Kate to a Kate
Conformable as other household Kates.
Here comes your father: never make denial;[9]
I must and will have Katharine to my wife.

    Re-enter BAPTISTA, GREMIO, *and* TRANIO C.[10]

    BAPTISTA. Now, Signior Petruchio, how speed you with my daughter?
    PETRUCHIO. How but well, sir? how but well?
It were impossible I should speed amiss.[11]
    BAPTISTA. Why, how now, daughter Katharine! in your dumps?
    KATHARINA. Call you me daughter? now, I promise you
You have show'd a tender fatherly regard,
To wish me wed to one half lunatic;[12]
A madcap ruffian and a swearing Jack,
That thinks with oaths to face the matter out.
    PETRUCHIO.[13] Father, 'tis thus: yourself and all the world,
That talk'd of her, have talk'd amiss of her:
If she be curst, it is for policy,
For she's not froward, but modest as the dove;
She is not hot, but temperate as the morn;
For patience she will prove a second Grissel,
And Roman Lucrece for her chastity;
And to conclude, we have 'greed so well together,
That upon Sunday is the wedding-day.
    KATHARINA. I'll see thee hang'd on Sunday first.
    GREMIO. Hark, Petruchio; she says she'll see thee hang'd first.
    TRANIO. Is this your speeding? nay, then, good night our part!
    PETRUCHIO. Be patient, gentlemen; I choose her for myself;
If she and I be pleased, what's that to you?

'Tis bargain'd 'twixt us twain, being alone,
That she shall still be curst in company.
I tell you, 'tis incredible to believe
How much she loves me: O, the kindest Kate!
She hung about my neck; and kiss on kiss
She vied so fast, protesting oath on oath,
That in a twink she won me to her love.
O, you are novices! 'tis a world to see,
How tame, when men and women are alone,
A meacock wretch can make the curstest shrew.
[1] Give me thy hand, Kate: I will unto Venice,
To buy apparel 'gainst the wedding-day.
Provide the feast, father, and bid the guests;
I will be sure my Katharine shall be fine.
    BAPTISTA. I know not what to say: but give me your hands; [2]
God send you joy, Petruchio! 'tis a match.
    GREMIO, TRANIO. Amen, say we: we will be witnesses.
    PETRUCHIO. Father, and wife, and gentlemen, adieu;
I will to Venice; Sunday comes apace:
We will have rings and things and fine array; [3]
And kiss me, Kate, we will be married o' Sunday. [4]

   [*Exeunt* KATHARINA *and* PETRUCHIO *severally.*[5]

    GREMIO. Was ever match clapp'd up so suddenly?
    BAPTISTA. Faith, gentlemen, now I play a merchant's part,
And venture madly on a desperate mart.
    TRANIO. 'Twas a commodity lay fretting by you:
'Twill bring you gain, or perish on the seas.
    BAPTISTA. The gain I seek is, quiet in the match.
    GREMIO. No doubt but he hath got a quiet catch.
But now, Baptista, to your younger daughter:
Now is the day we long have looked for:
I am your neighbour, and was suitor first.
    TRANIO. And I am one that love Bianca more [6]
Than words can witness, or your thoughts can guess.
    GREMIO. Youngling, thou canst not love so dear as I. [7]
    TRANIO. Greybeard, thy love doth freeze.
    GREMIO.   But thine doth fry.
Skipper, stand back: 'tis age that nourisheth.
    TRANIO. But youth in ladies' eyes that flourisheth.
    BAPTISTA.[8] Content you, gentlemen: I will compound this strife:
'Tis deeds must win the prize; and he of both
That can assure my daughter greatest dower
Shall have my Bianca's love.[9]
Say, Signior Gremio, what can you assure her?
    GREMIO. First, as you know, my house within the city
Is richly furnished with plate and gold;
Basins and ewers to lave her dainty hands;
My hangings all of Tyrian tapestry;
In ivory coffers I have stuff'd my crowns;
In cypress chests my arras, counterpoints,
Costly apparel, tents, and canopies,
Fine linen, Turkey cushions boss'd with pearl,
Valance of Venice gold in needlework,
Pewter and brass and all things that belong
To house or housekeeping: then, at my farm
    C

[1] PETRUCHIO *crosses in front to* KATHARINA.

[2] PETRUCHIO *forces* KATHARINA *to give her hand with his to* BAPTISTA.

[3] PETRUCHIO *swings* KATHARINA *round to* C., *then kisses her.*
[4] KATHARINA *strikes him on the face with the flat of her hand and, mad with passion, runs out* C.
[5] GREMIO *and* TRANIO *go up stage and look after* PETRUCHIO, BAPTISTA *sits in chair by table* R. *Then* GREMIO *comes down stage to* BAPTISTA'S *left as he speaks to him.*

[6] TRANIO *crosses* GREMIO *to* BAPTISTA.

[7] GREMIO *coming between* TRANIO *and* BAPTISTA *causes* TRANIO *to step back to* C. *down stage.* BAPTISTA *rises and fetches chair from up stage* R.

[8] *Coming between them with chair.*

[9] *Motioning them to sit* R *and* L. BAPTISTA C., GREMIO R., TRANIO L.

I have a hundred milch-kine to the pail,
Six score fat oxen standing in my stalls,
And all things answerable to this portion.
Myself am struck in years, I must confess;
And if I die to-morrow, this is hers,
If whilst I live she will be only mine.
TRANIO. That *only* came well in. Sir, list to me:
I am my father's heir and only son;
If I may have your daughter to my wife,
I'll leave her houses three or four as good,
Within rich Pisa walls, as any one
Old Signior Gremio has in Padua;
Besides two thousand ducats by the year
Of fruitful land, all which shall be her jointure.
What, have I pinch'd you, Signior Gremio?
GREMIO. Two thousand ducats by the year of land!
My land amounts not to so much in all:
That she shall have; besides an argosy
That now is lying in Marseilles' road.
What, have I choked you with an argosy?
TRANIO. Gremio, 'tis known my father hath no less
Than three great argosies; besides two galliases,
And twelve tight galleys: these I will assure her,
And twice as much, whate'er thou offer'st next
GREMIO. Nay, I have offer'd all, I have no more;
And she can have no more than all I have:
If you like me, she shall have me and mine.
TRANIO. Why, then the maid is mine from all the world,
By your firm promise: Gremio is out-vied.
BAPTISTA. I must confess your offer is the best;
And, let your father make her the assurance,
She is your own; else, you must pardon me,
If you should die before him, where's her dower?
TRANIO. That's but a cavil: he is old, I young,
GREMIO.[1] And may not young men die, as well as old?
BAPTISTA.[2] Well, gentlemen,
I am thus resolved: on Sunday next you know
My daughter Katharine is to be married:
Now, on the Sunday following, shall Bianca
Be bride to you, if you make this assurance;
If not, to Signior Gremio:
And so, I take my leave, and thank you both.
GREMIO. Adieu, good neighbour. [*Exit* BAPTISTA C.
　　　　　　　　　　　　　　Now I fear thee not:
Sirrah young gamester, your father were a fool
To give thee all, and in his waning age
Set foot under thy table: tut, a toy!
An old Italian fox is not so kind, my boy. [*Exit* C.
TRANIO. A vengeance on your crafty wither'd hide!
Yet I have faced it with a card of ten.
'Tis in my head to do my master good:
I see no reason but supposed Lucentio
Must get a father, call'd *supposed Vincentio*;
And that's a wonder: fathers commonly
Do get their children; but in this case of wooing,
A child shall get a sire, if I fail not of my cunning.
　　　　　　　　　　　　　　　　　　　　[*Exit* C.

[1] *Rising.*
[2] *Rising, placing chair on one side as he speaks.*

At the end of the scene, should the furniture in the course of the action have been moved too far down stage, PLAYERS' BOYS draw it up stage so that Traverse No. 2 can be drawn across. After it is drawn two BOYS carry on from R. and place C. a trellis arbour to seat two : this should be covered with leaves. The BOYS exeunt the way they enter. Then enter from R. down stage as before PLAYERS' BOY with Location Card " Baptista's Garden." He retires same entrance. All should be done quickly and neatly. Space should be left for characters to pass behind arbour.

SCENE VI

Padua. BAPTISTA'S *garden.*

Enter L., HORTENSIO, *and* BIANCA, *followed by* LUCENTIO.[1]

LUCENTIO. Fiddler, forbear ; you grow too forward, sir :
Have you so soon forgot the entertainment
Her sister Katharine welcomed you withal ?

HORTENSIO.[2] But, wrangling pedant, this is
The patroness of heavenly harmony :
Then give me leave to have prerogative ;
And when in music we have spent an hour,
Your lecture shall have leisure for as much.[3]

LUCENTIO. Preposterous ass, that never read so far
To know the cause why music was ordain'd !
Was it not to refresh the mind of man
After his studies or his usual pain ?
Then give me leave to read philosophy.
And while I pause, serve in your harmony.

HORTENSIO. Sirrah, I will not bear these braves of thine.

BIANCA.[4] Why, gentlemen, you do me double wrong,
To strive for that which resteth in my choice :
I am no breeching scholar in the schools ;
I'll not be tied to hours nor 'pointed times,
But learn my lessons as I please myself.
And, to cut off all strife,[5] here sit we down ;
Take you your instrument, play you the whiles ;
His lecture will be done ere you have tuned.

HORTENSIO. You'll leave his lecture when I am in tune ?

LUCENTIO. That will be never : tune your instrument.[6]

BIANCA. Where left we last ?

LUCENTIO.   Here, madam :
*Hic ibat Simois ; hic est Sigeia tellus ;
Hic steterat Priami regia celsa senis.*

BIANCA. Construe them.[7]

LUCENTIO.[8] *Hic ibat,* as I told you before,[9] *Simois,* I am Lucentio,[9]
hic est, son unto Vincentio of Pisa,[9] *Sigeia tellus,* disguised thus to get
your love ;[9] *Hic steterat,* and that Lucentio that comes a-wooing,[9]
Priami, is my man Tranio,[9] *regia,* bearing my port,[9] *celsa senis,* that
we might beguile the old pantaloon.

HORTENSIO.[10] Madam, my instrument's in tune.

BIANCA. Let's hear.[11] O fie ! the treble jars.

LUCENTIO. Spit in the hole, man, and tune again.[12]

BIANCA. Now let me see if I can construe it :[13]
Hic ibat Simois, I know you not, *hic est Sigeia tellus,* I trust you not ;
Hic steterat Priami, take heed he hear us not,[14] *regia,* presume not,[15]
celsa senis, despair not.

[1] HORTENSIO, *who carries a lute, is on* BIANCA'S *right ; preceding her, he leads her to arbour, she sits on seat in arbour. As* HORTENSIO *seats himself beside her* LUCENTIO, *who has been watching* HORTENSIO, *comes across stage to* R. *behind arbour and speaks.*

[2] *Jumping up.*

[3] *Position.*   BIANCA.
   LUCENTIO.   HORTENSIO.

[4] *Rising.*

[5] *To* LUCENTIO. LUCENTIO *takes her hand and they sit.*

[6] HORTENSIO *moves up stage watching* LUCENTIO *and gets behind the arbour.* BIANCA *and* LUCENTIO *sit in arbour.*

[7] *They look round to see if* HORTENSIO *is in sight.*
[8] *The Latin is spoken loudly and construed as asides to* BIANCA.
[9] HORTENSIO *twangs on his lute, each twang in comic emphasis.*

[10] *Coming forward* L. *of arbour*
[11] *Sounding a few strings.*

[12] HORTENSIO *retires in anger behind arbour*
[13] BIANCA *and* LUCENTIO *get very close together.*
[14] *They peep round.* LUCENTIO *puts his arm round* BIANCA'S *waist.*
[15] *Removing* LUCENTIO'S *arm from her waist.*

[left margin notes:]

¹ Coming forward.

² LUCENTIO rises.

³ Crossing to LUCENTIO.

⁴ HORTENSIO turns to BIANCA and kneels.

⁵ Taking a paper from his pocket.

⁶ Striking a love-lorn attitude.

⁷ Rising.

⁸ Letting gamut fall to the ground and circling to R. of arbour. HORTENSIO turns on his knees.

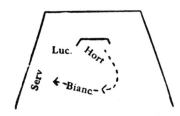

HORTENSIO.¹ Madam, 'tis now in tune.

LUCENTIO. All but the base.

HORTENSIO. The base is right; 'tis the base knave that jars.
[*Aside*] How fiery and forward our pedant is!
Now, for my life, the knave doth court my love:
Pedascule, I'll watch you better yet.

BIANCA. In time I may believe, yet I mistrust.

LUCENTIO. Mistrust it not; for, sure, Æacides
Was Ajax, call'd so from his grandfather.

BIANCA. I must believe my master; else, I promise you,
I should be arguing still upon that doubt:
But let it rest. Now, Licio, to you: ²
Good masters, take it not unkindly, pray,
That I have been thus pleasant with you both.

HORTENSIO.³ You may go walk, and give me leave a while:
My lessons make no music in three parts.

LUCENTIO. Are you so formal, sir? ⁴ well, I must wait,
[*Aside*] And watch withal; for, but I be deceived,
Our fine musician groweth amorous.

HORTENSIO. Madam, before you touch the instrument,
To learn the order of my fingering,
I must begin with rudiments of art;
To teach you gamut in a briefer sort,
More pleasant, pithy and effectual,
Than hath been taught by any of my trade:
And there it is in writing, fairly drawn.⁵

BIANCA. Why, I am past my gamut long ago.

HORTENSIO. Yet read the gamut of Hortensio.⁶

BIANCA [*reads*]. Gamut *I am, the ground of all accord,*
    A re, *to plead Hortensio's passion;*
    B mi, *Bianca, take him for thy lord,*
        C fa ut, *that loves with all affection:*
    D sol re, *one clef, two notes have I;*
    E la mi, *show pity, or I die.*⁷
Call you this gamut? tut, I like it not: ⁸
Old fashions please me best; I am not so nice,
To change true rules for old inventions.

Enter a SERVANT R.⁹

SERVANT. Mistress, your father prays you leave your books
And help to dress your sister's chamber up:
You know to-morrow is the wedding-day.

BIANCA. Farewell, sweet masters both; I must be gone.
[*Exeunt* BIANCA *and* SERVANT R.

LUCENTIO. Faith, mistress, then I have no cause to stay.
[*Exit* R.

HORTENSIO. But I have cause to pry into this pedant:
Methinks he looks as though he were in love:
Yet if thy thoughts, Bianca, be so humble,
To cast thy wandering eyes on every stale,
Seize thee that list: if once I find thee ranging,
Hortensio will be quit with thee by changing.

[*Exit* R.

BOYS *enter and remove arbour* L. *Traverse No.* 2 *drawn off. No
Location Card necessary here. Characters entering on next scene as
Traverse is drawn.*

SCENE VII

Padua. BAPTISTA'S *house.*

Enter BAPTISTA, GREMIO, TRANIO, KATHARINA, BIANCA, LUCENTIO, *and others,* ATTENDANTS C.[1]

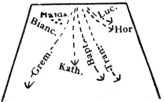

Order of entrance to positions at Diagram. TRANIO *followed by* BAPTISTA *to down* L. *and* L.C. *respectively.* HORTENSIO *and* LUCENTIO *to up stage* L. KATHARINA *to* C. GREMIO *to* R. *down stage.* BIANCA, MAIDS *and* SERVANTS (*if used*) *to up* R.

[1] *Sitting chair* L.

[2] *Coming forward.*

BAPTISTA [*to* TRANIO]. Signior Lucentio, this is the 'pointed day
That Katharine and Petruchio should be married,
And yet we hear not of our son-in-law.
What will be said ? what mockery will it be,
To want the bridegroom when the priest attends
To speak the ceremonial rites of marriage !
What says Lucentio to this shame of ours ?[2]
KATHARINA.[3] No shame but mine : I must, forsooth, be forced
To give my hand opposed against my heart
Unto a mad-brain rudesby full of spleen ;
Who woo'd in haste and means to wed at leisure.[4]
I told you, I, he was a frantic fool,
Hiding his bitter jests in blunt behaviour :
And, to be noted for a merry man,
He'll woo a thousand, 'point the day of marriage,
Make feasts, invite friends, and proclaim the banns ;
Yet never means to wed where he hath woo'd.
Now must the world point at poor Katharine,
And say, *Lo, there is mad Petruchio's wife,*
If it would please him come and marry her[5]
TRANIO.[6] Patience, good Katharine, and Baptista too.
Upon my life, Petruchio means but well,
Whatever fortune stays him from his word :
Though he be blunt, I know him passing wise ;
Though he be merry, yet withal he's honest.
KATHARINA. Would Katharine had never seen him though !
                    [*Exit weeping down stage door* R.
BAPTISTA.[7] Go, girl ; I cannot blame thee now to weep ;
For such an injury would vex a very saint,
Much more a shrew of thy impatient humour.

[3] BAPTISTA *makes a sympathetic gesture to her, but is repelled by* KATHARINA'S *tone.* " *I told you, I* "

[5] *Turns to* R.C. BAPTISTA *rises.*

[6] *Crossing to* C.

[7] *Crossing* R.

Enter BIONDELLO.[8]

BIONDELLO. Master, master ! news, old news, and such news as
you never heard of !
BAPTISTA. Is it new and old too ? how may that be ?
BIONDELLO. Why, is it not news, to hear of Petruchio's coming ?
BAPTISTA. Is he come ?
BIONDELLO. Why, no, sir.
BAPTISTA. What then ?
BIONDELLO. He is coming.
BAPTISTA. When will he be here ?
BIONDELLO. When he stands where I am and sees you there.
TRANIO. But say, what to thine old news ?
BIONDELLO. Why, Petruchio is coming in a new hat and an old
jerkin, a pair of old breeches thrice turned, a pair of boots that have
been candle-cases, one buckled, another laced, an old rusty sword
ta'en out of the town-armoury, with a broken hilt, and chapeless ;
with two broken points : his horse hipped with an old mothy saddle
and stirrups of no kindred ; besides, possessed with the glanders and
like to mose in the chine ; troubled with the lampass, infected with the
fashions, full of windgalls, sped with spavins, rayed with the yellows,

[8] *He enters* C. *from* L. *and comes to* C.

past cure of the fives, stark spoiled with the staggers, begnawn with the bots, swayed in the back and shoulder-shotten ; near-legged before and with a half-checked bit and a head-stall of sheep's leather which, being restrained to keep him from stumbling, hath been often burst and now repaired with knots ; one girth six times pieced and a woman's crupper of velure, which hath two letters for her name fairly set down in studs, and here and there pieced with packthread.

BAPTISTA. Who comes with him ?

BIONDELLO. O, sir, his lackey, for all the world caparisoned like the horse ; with a linen stock on one leg and a kersey boot-hose on the other, gartered with a red and blue list ; an old hat and *the humour of forty fancies* pricked in't for a feather : a monster, a very monster in apparel, and not like a Christian footboy or a gentleman's lackey.

TRANIO. 'Tis some odd humour pricks him to this fashion ;
Yet oftentimes he goes but mean-apparell'd.

BAPTISTA. I am glad he's come, howsoe'er he comes.

BIONDELLO. Why, sir, he comes not.

BAPTISTA. Didst thou not say he comes ?

BIONDELLO. Who ? that Petruchio came ?

BAPTISTA. Ay, that Petruchio came.

BIONDELLO. No, sir ; I say his horse comes, with him on his back.

BAPTISTA. Why, that's all one.

BIONDELLO.[1] Nay, by Saint Jamy,
    I hold you a penny,
    A horse and a man
    Is more than one,
    And yet not many.

Enter PETRUCHIO *and* GRUMIO C [2]

PETRUCHIO. Come, where be these gallants ? who's at home ?

BAPTISTA. You are welcome, sir.

PETRUCHIO. And yet I come not well.

BAPTISTA. And yet you halt not.

TRANIO.   Not so well apparell'd
As I wish you were.

PETRUCHIO. Were it better, I should rush in thus.
But where is Kate ? where is my lovely bride ?
How does my father ? Gentles, methinks you frown :
And wherefore gaze this goodly company,
As if they saw some wondrous monument,
Some comet or unusual prodigy ? [3]

BAPTISTA. Why, sir, you know this is your wedding-day :
First were we sad, fearing you would not come ;
Now sadder, that you come so unprovided.
Fie, doff this habit, shame to your estate,
An eye-sore to our solemn festival !

TRANIO. And tell us, what occasion of import
Hath all so long detain'd you from your wife,
And sent you hither so unlike yourself ?

PETRUCHIO. Tedious it were to tell, and harsh to hear :
Sufficeth, I am come to keep my word,
Though in some part enforced to digress ;
Which, at more leisure, I will so exc se
As you shall well be satisfied withal.
But where is Kate ? I stay too long from her :
The morning wears, 'tis time we were at church.

[1] *Getting behind chair* L. *as* BAPTISTA *is getting angry. If in this business the chair is moved below Traverse 2,* BION- DELLO *can protectingly drag it above and clear it for the next scene.*

[2] *They pose up stage* C. *in their ragged array.*

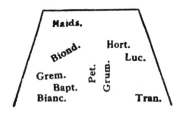

Maids.
Biond.   Hort.
         Luc.
Grem.   Pet. Grum.
  Bapt.
Bianc.   Tran.

TRANIO. See not your bride in these unreverent robes:
Go to my chamber ; put on clothes of mine.

PETRUCHIO. Not I, believe me : thus I'll visit her.

BAPTISTA. But thus, I trust, you will not marry her.

PETRUCHIO. Good sooth, even thus ; therefore ha' done with
  words :
To me she's married, not unto my clothes :
Could I repair what she will wear in me,
As I can change these poor accoutrements,
'Twere well for Kate and better for myself.
But what a fool am I to chat with you,
When I should bid good morrow to my bride,
And seal the title with a lovely kiss !
                    [*Exeunt* PETRUCHIO *and* GRUMIO.[1]

TRANIO. He hath some meaning in his mad attire : [2]
We will persuade him, be it possible,
To put on better ere he go to church.

BAPTISTA. I'll after him, and see the event of this.
    [*Exeunt* BAPTISTA *and* GREMIO, *followed by all but* TRANIO *and*
                                          LUCENTIO.[3]

SCENE VIII.

BAPTISTA'S *garden.*

TRANIO. But to her love concerneth us to add
Her father's liking : which to bring to pass,
As I before imparted to your worship,
I am to get a man,—whate'er he be,
It skills not much, we'll fit him to our turn,—
And he shall be Vincentio of Pisa ;
And make assurance here in Padua
Of greater sums than I have promised.
So shall you quietly enjoy your hope,
And marry sweet Bianca with consent.

LUCENTIO. Were it not that my fellow-schoolmaster
Doth watch Bianca's steps so narrowly,
'Twere good, methinks, to steal our marriage ;
Which once perform'd, let all the world say no,
I'll keep mine own, despite of all the world.

TRANIO. That by degrees we mean to look into,
And watch our vantage in this business :
We'll over-reach the greybeard, Gremio,
The narrow-prying father, Minola,
The quaint musician, amorous Licio ;
All for my master's sake, Lucentio.

Re-enter GREMIO R.

Signior Gremio, came you from the church ?

GREMIO. As willingly as e'er I came from school.

TRANIO. And is the bride and bridegroom coming home ?

GREMIO. A bridegroom say you ? 'tis a groom indeed,
A grumbling groom, and that the girl shall find.

TRANIO. Curster than she ? why, 'tis impossible.

GREMIO. Why, he's a devil, a devil, a very fiend.

TRANIO. Why, she's a devil, a devil, the devil's dam.

GREMIO. Tut, she's a lamb, a dove, a fool to him !
I'll tell you, Sir Lucentio : when the priest
Should ask, if Katharine should be his wife,

[1] *Down stage door* R.

[2] *At the exit of* PETRUCHIO *and* GRUMIO, *all
move as indicated in diagram and subsequently pass off in the order of their
nearness to the door* R.

[3] *As the exit is made Traverse No. 2 is
drawn over.* TRANIO *moves to* LUCENTIO
L. *During general exit inviting him to
stay. Speaks when Traverse is drawn
behind them.*

Ay, by gogs-wouns, quoth he ; and swore so loud,
That, all-amazed, the priest let fall the book ;
And, as he stoop'd again to take it up,
The mad-brain'd bridegroom took him such a cuff
That down fell priest and book and book and priest :
Now take them up, quoth he, *if any list.*
    TRANIO.   What said the wench when he rose again ?
    GREMIO.   Trembled and shook ; for why, he stamp'd and swore,
As if the vicar meant to cozen him.
But after many ceremonies done,
He calls for wine : *A health !* quoth he, as if
He had been aboard, carousing to his mates
After a storm : quaff'd off the muscadel
And threw the sops all in the sexton's face ;
Having no other reason
But that his beard grew thin and hungerly
And seem'd to ask him sops as he was drinking.
This done, he took the bride about the neck
And kiss'd her lips with such a clamorous smack
That at the parting all the church did echo :
And I seeing this came thence for very shame ;
And after me, I know, the rout is coming.
Such a mad marriage never was before :
Hark, hark ! I hear the minstrels play.[1]

                                 [Music approaching.

SCENE IX.

BAPTISTA'S *house.*

Re-enter PETRUCHIO, KATHARINA, BIANCA, BAPTISTA, HORTENSIO,
GRUMIO, MAIDS, GUESTS *and* SERVANTS R.[2]

    PETRUCHIO.   Gentlemen and friends, I thank you for your pains :
I know you think to dine with me to-day,
And have prepared great store of wedding cheer ;
But so it is, my haste doth call me hence,
And therefore here I mean to take my leave.
    BAPTISTA.   Is't possible you will away to-night ?
    PETRUCHIO.   I must away to-day, before night come :
Make it no wonder ; if you knew my business,
You would entreat me rather go than stay.
And, honest company, I thank you all,
That have beheld me give away myself
To this most patient, sweet and virtuous wife :
Dine with my father, drink a health to me ;
For I must hence ; and farewell to you all.
    TRANIO.   Let us entreat you stay till after dinner.
    PETRUCHIO.   It may not be.
    GREMIO.   Let me entreat you.
    PETRUCHIO.   It cannot be.
    KATHARINA.   Let me entreat you.
    PETRUCHIO.   I am content.
    KATHARINA.   Are you content to stay ?
    PETRUCHIO.   I am content you shall entreat me stay ;
But yet not stay, entreat me how you can.
    KATHARINA.   Now, if you love me, stay.
    PETRUCHIO.   Grumio, my horse.
    GRUMIO.   Ay, sir, they be ready : the oats have eaten the horses.

[1] *Traverse drawn off.* GREMIO *moves* R. *into scene.* LUCENTIO *and* TRANIO L. *up stage.*

[2] *The positions of diagram are reached as follows.*
The procession is headed by the musicians playing, who march across stage from R. *entrance to* L.C., *turn and go to* R. *corner of stage and group themselves. The* BRIDESMAIDS *follow them, stopping* R.C., *forming a lane. This business must be timed to finish as musicians group* R. BAPTISTA *follows, leading* BIANCA, *they pass through the lane turning out of it and getting* R.C. *down stage.* HORTENSIO *follows in front of* GUESTS, *who with him get* L. *and form group.* SERVANTS *and* PAGES *and* BIONDELLO *now pass behind maids to* L. *and* R. *up stage.* PETRUCHIO *leading* KATHARINA *through lane to* C. GRUMIO *behind* PETRUCHIO *gets on his* L. *Musicians stop as* PETRUCHIO *speaks.*

KATHARINA. Nay, then,
Do what thou canst, I will not go to-day ;
No, nor to-morrow, not till I please myself.
The door is open, sir ; there lies your way ;
You may be jogging whiles your boots are green ;
For me, I'll not be gone till I please myself :
'Tis like you'll prove a jolly surly groom,
That take it on you at the first so roundly.
    PETRUCHIO. O Kate, content thee ; prithee, be not angry.
    KATHARINA. I will be angry : what hast thou to do ?
[1] Father, be quiet : he shall stay my leisure.
    GREMIO. Ay, marry, sir, now it begins to work.
    KATHARINA. Gentlemen, forward to the bridal dinner :
I see a woman may be made a fool,
If she had not a spirit to resist.
    PETRUCHIO. They shall go forward, Kate, at thy command.
Obey the bride, you that attend on her ;
Go to the feast, revel and domineer,
Carouse full measure to her maidenhead,
Be mad and merry, or go hang yourselves : [2]
But for my bonny Kate, she must with me.[3]
Nay, look not big, nor stamp, nor stare, nor fret ;
I will be master of what is mine own : [4]
She is my goods, my chattels ; she is my house,
My household stuff, my field, my barn,
My horse, my ox, my ass, my any thing ;
And here she stands, touch her whoever dare ;
I'll bring mine action on the proudest he
That stops my way in Padua. Grumio,
Draw forth thy weapon, we are beset with thieves ;
Rescue thy mistress, if thou be a man.[5]
Fear not, sweet wench, they shall not touch thee, Kate : [6]
I'll buckler thee against a million.[7]

SCENE X.[8]

BAPTISTA'S *garden.*

BAPTISTA. Nay, let them go, a couple of quiet ones.
GREMIO. Went they not quickly, I should die with laughing.
TRANIO. Of all mad matches never was the like.
LUCENTIO. Mistress, what's your opinion of your sister ?
BIANCA. That, being mad herself, she's madly mated.
GREMIO. I warrant him, Petruchio is Kated.
BAPTISTA. Neighbours and friends, though bride and bridegroom
    wants
For to supply the places at the table,
You know there wants no junkets at the feast.
Lucentio, you shall supply the bridegroom's place ;
And let Bianca take her sister's room.
    TRANIO. Shall sweet Bianca practise how to bride it ?
    BAPTISTA. She shall, Lucentio. Come, gentlemen, let's go.
                           [*Exeunt* L..[9]

[1] BAPTISTA *has made no movement.*

[2] *Under pressure of* PETRUCHIO'S *assumed violence the whole of the company* L., *i.e.,* SERVANTS, TRANIO, LUCENTIO, HORTENSIO *and* GUESTS *escape over to* R., *leaving* PETRUCHIO, KATHARINA *and* GRUMIO L.
[3] *Grasping* KATHARINA *by wrist.*
[4] *Swinging* KATHARINA *over* L.

[5] GRUMIO *draws sword crossing to* O.

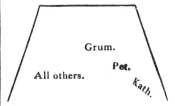

[6] *Swinging* KATHARINA *up stage.* GRUMIO *to* R.C. *above group.*
[7] *Throwing* KATHARINA *over his shoulder he exits* O. *to* R., *followed by* GRUMIO, *waving his sword followed by the Company. At general exit,* SLY, *who has awaked during the marriage scene, gets excited and follows the general exit, but collapses* O. *The* LORD *motions the* PAGE *dressed as a lady, who throws* SLY *over his shoulder mimicing* PETRUCHIO'S *exit with* KATHARINA.
[8] *Traverse No. 2 drawn on. Enter* PETRUCHIO *with* KATHARINA *on shoulder, crosses from* R. *to* L., *and exit.* GRUMIO *follows backward, waving sword. Exit.* TRANIO, BAPTISTA, GREMIO *follow and stand* L. *looking out as though following* KATHARINA *and* PETRUCHIO *with their eyes.* LUCENTIO *and* BIANCA *stand* R. HORTENSIO O., GUESTS, *etc., grouped*

[9] *Players' Boy enters down* L. *with* "Interval" Card.
    Act Drop.

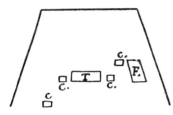

This scene is played on full stage. See Diagram for disposition of furniture. T—Table.   F—Fire.   C—Chair. Players' Boy enters R. as before with Location Card, "Petruchio's Country House." He retires same entrance.
¹ *Moving round table from R. to L. as he speaks.*
² *Yawning and sitting L.*
³ *Rising quickly.*

⁴ *Crosses to GRUMIO.*

⁵ *CURTIS crosses to Fire.*

⁶ *CURTIS kneels and blows fire.*

⁷ *Rising and coming to GRUMIO.*

⁸ *Sitting by fire warming hands.*

⁹ *Rising, walking CURTIS backwards to C.*

¹¹ *Sitting on table. CURTIS follows.*

PART II.

SCENE I

ᴘᴇᴛʀᴜᴄʜɪᴏ's *house.*¹

Enter GRUMIO C. *from* L.

²GRUMIO.   Fie, fie on all tired jades, on all mad masters, and all foul ways !   Was ever man so beaten ? was ever man so rayed ? was ever man so weary ? ³ I am sent before to make a fire, and they are coming after to warm them.   Now, were not I a little pot and soon hot, my very lips might freeze to my teeth, my tongue to the roof of my mouth, my heart in my belly, ere I should come by a fire to thaw me : but I, with blowing the fire, shall warm myself ; for, considering the weather, a taller man than I will take cold.⁴ Holla, ho ! Curtis.

Enter CURTIS R.

CURTIS.   Who is that calls so coldly ? ⁵

GRUMIO.   A piece of ice : if thou doubt it, thou mayst slide from my shoulder to my heel with no greater a run but my head and my neck.   A fire, good Curtis.

CURTIS.   Is my master and his wife coming, Grumio ?

GRUMIO.   O, ay, Curtis, ay : and therefore fire, fire ; ⁶ cast on no water.

CURTIS.   Is she so hot a shrew as she's reported ?

GRUMIO.   She was, good Curtis, before this frost : but, thou knowest, winter tames man, woman and beast ; for it hath tamed my old master and my new mistress and myself, fellow Curtis.   But wilt thou make a fire ⁷ or shall I complain on thee to our mistress, whose hand, she being now at hand, thou shalt soon feel, to thy cold comfort, for being slow in thy hot office ?

CURTIS.   I prithee, good Grumio, tell me, how goes the world ?

GRUMIO.   A cold world, Curtis, in every office but thine ; and therefore fire : do thy duty, and have thy duty ; for my master and mistress are almost frozen to death.

CURTIS.   There's fire ready ; ⁸ and therefore, good Grumio, the news.

GRUMIO.   Why, *Jack, boy ! ho ! boy !* and as much news as will thaw.⁹

CURTIS.   Come, you are so full of coney-catching !

GRUMIO.   Why, therefore fire ; for I have caught extreme cold.¹⁰ Where's the cook ? is supper ready, the house trimmed, rushes strewed, cobwebs swept ; the serving-men in their new fustian, their white stockings, and every officer his wedding-garment on ?   Be the jacks fair within, the jills fair without, the carpets laid, and everything in order ?

CURTIS.   All ready ; and therefore, I pray thee, news.

GRUMIO.¹¹   First, know, my horse is tired ; my master and mistress fallen out.

CURTIS.   How ?

GRUMIO.   Out of their saddles into the dirt ; and thereby hangs a tale.

CURTIS.   Let's ha't, good Grumio.

GRUMIO.   Lend thine ear.

CURTIS.   Here.

GRUMIO.   There.   [*Strikes him.*

CURTIS.   This is to feel a tale, not to hear a tale.

GRUMIO.   And therefore 'tis called a sensible tale : and this cuff was but to knock at your ear, and beseech listening.   Now I begin :

Imprimis, we came down a foul hill, my master riding behind my mistress,—

CURTIS. Both of one horse ?

GRUMIO. What's that to thee ?

CURTIS. Why, a horse.

GRUMIO.[1] Tell thou the tale : but hadst thou not crossed me, thou shouldst have heard how her horse fell and she under her horse ; thou shouldst have heard in how miry a place, how she was bemoiled, how he left her with the horse upon her, how he beat me because her horse stumbled, how she waded through the dirt to pluck him off me, how he swore, how she prayed, that never prayed before, how I cried, how the horses ran away, how her bridle was burst, how I lost my crupper, with many things of worthy memory, which now shall die in oblivion and thou return unexperienced to thy grave.

CURTIS. By this reckoning he is more shrew than she.

GRUMIO. Ay ; and that thou and the proudest of you all shall find when he comes home.[2] But what talk I of this ? Call forth Nathaniel, Joseph, Nicholas, Philip, Walter, Sugarsop and the rest : let their heads be sleekly combed, their blue coats brushed and their garters of an indifferent knit : let them curtsy with their left legs and not presume to touch a hair of my master's horse-tail till they kiss their hands. Are they all ready ?

CURTIS. They are.

GRUMIO. Call them forth.

CURTIS. Do you hear, ho ?[3] you must meet my master to countenance my mistress.

GRUMIO. Why, she hath a face of her own.

CURTIS. Who knows not that ?

GRUMIO. Thou, it seems, that calls for company to countenance her.

CURTIS. I call them forth to credit her.

GRUMIO. Why, she comes to borrow nothing of them.

Enter four or five SERVINGMEN.[4]

NATHANIEL. Welcome home, Grumio !

PHILIP. How now, Grumio !

JOSEPH. What, Grumio !

NICHOLAS. Fellow Grumio !

NATHANIEL. How now, old lad ?

GRUMIO. Welcome, you ;—how now, you ;—what, you ;—fellow, you ;[5]—and thus much for greeting. Now, my spruce companions, is all ready, and all things neat ?

NATHANIEL. All things is ready. How near is our master ?

GRUMIO. E'en at hand, alighted by this ; and therefore be not[6]— Cock's passion, silence ! I hear my master.

Enter PETRUCHIO *dragging* KATHARINA *dressed in a dirty copy of her wedding attire* C.

PETRUCHIO. Where be these knaves ?[7] What, no man at door To hold my stirrup nor to take my horse ! Where is Nathaniel, Gregory, Philip ?

ALL SERVANTS.[8] Here, here, sir ; here, sir.

PETRUCHIO.[9] Here, sir ! here, sir ! here, sir ! here, sir ! You logger-headed and unpolish'd grooms ! What, no attendance ? no regard ? no duty ? Where is the foolish knave I sent before ?

GRUMIO.[10] Here, sir ; as foolish as I was before.

[1] *Getting off table, crossing round back and sitting* R. *of table.*

[2] *Rising.*

[3] *Moving to back* C.

[4] *Running to* GRUMIO C., *and surrounding him.*

[5] *Pushing them away.*

[6] PETRUCHIO *heard off stage.* GRUMIO *gets under table* C. SERVANTS *run through door* R.

[7] *Coming* C., *dragging* KATHARINA *with him*

[8] *They just appear one by one.*

[9] *Whipping them into a row at back of table, following them, dragging* KATHARINA *with him.*

[10] *Peeping from under table.*

PETRUCHIO.[1] You peasant swain! you whoreson malt-horse drudge!
[2] Did I not bid thee meet me in the park,
And bring along these rascal knaves with thee?

GRUMIO. Nathaniel's coat, sir, was not fully made,
And Gabriel's pumps were all unpink'd i' the heel;
There was no link to colour Peter's hat,
And Walter's dagger was not come from sheathing:
There were none fine but Adam, Ralph, and Gregory;
The rest were ragged, old, and beggarly;
Yet, as they are, here are they come to meet you.

PETRUCHIO. Go, rascals, go, and fetch my supper in.
          [Exeunt SERVANTS C. *full of alacrity*
[Singing] *Where is the life that late I led*—
Where are those[3]—Sit down, Kate, and welcome.—
Soud, soud, soud, soud!

Re-enter SERVANTS *with supper.*[4]

Why, when, I say? Nay, good sweet Kate, be merry.
Off with my boots, you rogues! you villains, when?
[Sings] *It was the friar of orders grey,*
    As he forth walked on his way:—
Out, you rogue! you pluck my foot awry:
Take that, and mend the plucking off the other.
                          [Strikes him.

Be merry, Kate. Some water, here; what, ho![5]
Where's my spaniel Troilus? Sirrah, get you hence,[6]
And bid my cousin Ferdinand come hither:[7]
One, Kate, that you must kiss, and be acquainted with.
Where are my slippers? Shall I have some water?

[8]*Enter one with water.*

Come, Kate, and wash, and welcome heartily.
You whoreson villain! will you let it fall?
                          [Strikes him.

KATHARINA. Patience, I pray you; 'twas a fault unwilling.
PETRUCHIO. A whoreson, beetle-headed, flap-ear'd knave!
[9]Come, Kate, sit down,[10] I know you have a stomach.[11]
Will you give thanks, sweet Kate; or else shall I?[12]
[13]What's this? mutton?
FIRST SERVANT.   Ay.
PETRUCHIO.   Who brought it?
PETER.   I.
PETRUCHIO. 'Tis burnt; and so is all the meat.
What dogs are these! Where is the rascal cook?
How durst you, villains, bring it from the dresser,
And serve it thus to me that love it not?[14]
There, take it to you,[15] trenchers, cups, and all:
       [Throws the meat, etc., about the stage.
You heedless joltheads and unmanner'd slaves!
What, do you grumble? I'll be with you straight.
KATHARINA. I pray you, husband, be not so disquiet:
The meat was well, if you were so contented.
PETRUCHIO.[16] I tell thee, Kate, 'twas burnt and dried away;
And I expressly am forbid to touch it,
For it engenders choler, planteth anger;
And better 'twere that both of us did fast,

Since, of ourselves, ourselves are choleric,
Than feed it with such over-roasted flesh.
Be patient ; to-morrow 't shall be mended,
And, for this night, we'll fast for company : [1]
Come, I will bring thee to thy bridal chamber.[2]   [*Exeunt.*

Re-enter SERVANTS *severally.*

NATHANIEL. Peter, didst ever see the like ?
PETER. He kills her in her own humour.

Re-enter CURTIS.

GRUMIO. Where is he ?
CURTIS. In her chamber, making a sermon of continency to
her ;
And rails, and swears, and rates, that she, poor soul,
Knows not which way to stand, to look, to speak,
And sits as one new-risen from a dream.[3]
Away, away ! for he is coming hither.   [*Exeunt* C. *to* L.

Re-enter PETRUCHIO R.[4]

PETRUCHIO. Thus have I politicly begun my reign,
And 'tis my hope to end successfully.
My falcon now is sharp and passing empty ;
And till she stoop she must not be full-gorged,
For then she never looks upon her lure.
Another way I have to man my haggard,
To make her come and know her keeper's call,
That is, to watch her, as we watch these kites
That bate and beat and will not be obedient.
She eat no meat to-day, nor none shall eat ;
Last night she slept not, nor to-night she shall not ;
As with the meat, some undeserved fault
I'll find about the making of the bed ;
And here I'll fling the pillow, there the bolster,
This way the coverlet, another way the sheets :
Ay, and amid this hurly I intend
That all is done in reverend care of her ;
And in conclusion she shall watch all night :
And if she chance to nod I'll rail and brawl
And with the clamour keep her still awake.
This is a way to kill a wife with kindness ;
And thus I'll curb her mad and headstrong humour.
[5]He that knows better how to tame a shrew,
Now let him speak : 'tis charity to show.   [*Exit.*

Traverse No. 1 *or* 2 *drawn over.*

SCENE II

Padua. Near BAPTISTA'S *house.*[6]

Enter TRANIO *following* HORTENSIO R.

TRANIO. Is't possible, friend Licio, that Mistress Bianca
Doth fancy any other but Lucentio ?
I tell you, sir, she bears me fair in hand.
HORTENSIO. Sir, to satisfy you in what I have said,
Stand by and mark the manner of his teaching.[7]

Enter BIANCA *and* LUCENTIO *lovingly* R.

LUCENTIO. Now, mistress, profit you in what you read ?
BIANCA. What, master, read you ? first resolve me that.
LUCENTIO. I read that I profess, the Art to Love.
BIANCA. And may you prove, sir, master of your art ! [1]
LUCENTIO. While you, sweet dear, prove mistress of my heart ! [2]
                    [LUCENTIO *and* BIANCA *exeunt* L.
HORTENSIO.[3] Quick proceeders, marry ! Now, tell me, I pray,
You that durst swear that your mistress Bianca
Loved none in the world so well as Lucentio.
TRANIO. O despiteful love ! unconstant womankind !
I tell thee, Licio, this is wonderful.
HORTENSIO. Mistake no more : I am not Licio,
Nor a musician, as I seem to be ;
But one that scorn to live in this disguise,
For such a one as leaves a gentleman,
And makes a god of such a cullion :
Know, sir, that I am call'd Hortensio.[4]
TRANIO. Signior Hortensio, I have often heard
Of your entire affection to Bianca ;
And since mine eyes are witness of her lightness,
I will with you, if you be so contented,
Forswear Bianca and her love for ever.
HORTENSIO. See, how they kiss and court ! Signior Lucentio,
Here is my hand, and here I firmly vow
Never to woo her more, but do forswear her,
As one unworthy all the former favours
That I have fondly flatter'd her withal.
TRANIO. And here I take the like unfeigned oath,
Never to marry with her though she would entreat :
Fie on her ? see, how beastly she doth court him ?
HORTENSIO. Would all the world but he had quite forsworn !
For me, that I may surely keep mine oath,
I will be married to a wealthy widow,
Ere three days pass, which hath as long loved me
As I have loved this proud disdainful haggard.
And so farewell, Signior Lucentio.
Kindness in women, not their beauteous looks,
Shall win my love : and so I take my leave,
In resolutions as I swore before.   [Exit R.

Re-enter BIANCA *and* LUCENTIO.

TRANIO. Mistress Bianca, bless you with such grace
As 'longeth to a lover's blessed case !
Nay, I have ta'en you napping, gentle love,
And have forsworn you with Hortensio.
BIANCA. Tranio, you jest : but have you both forsworn me ?
TRANIO. Mistress, we have.
LUCENTIO.   Then we are rid of Licio.
TRANIO. I' faith, he'll have a lusty widow now,
That shall be woo'd and wedded in a day.
BIANCA. God give him joy !
TRANIO. Ay, and he'll tame her.
BIANCA.   He says so, Tranio.
TRANIO. Faith, he is gone unto the taming-school.
BIANCA. The taming-school ! what, is there such a place ?

TRANIO.   Ay, mistress, and Petruchio is the master;
That teacheth tricks eleven and twenty long,
To tame a shrew and charm her chattering tongue.[1]

Enter BIONDELLO L.

BIONDELLO.   O master, master, I have watch'd so long
That I am dog-weary: but at last I spied
An ancient angel coming down the hill,
Will serve the turn.
TRANIO.   What is he, Biondello?
BIONDELLO.   Master, a mercatante, or a pedant,
I know not what; but formal in apparel,
In gait and countenance surely like a father.
LUCENTIO.   And what of him, Tranio?
TRANIO.   If he be credulous and trust my tale,
I'll make him glad to seem Vincentio,
And give assurance to Baptista Minola,
As if he were the right Vincentio.
Take in your love, and then let me alone.
                    [*Exeunt* LUCENTIO *and* BIANCA R.

Enter a PEDANT L.[2]

PEDANT.   God save you, sir!
TRANIO.   And you, sir! you are welcome.
Travel you far on, or are you at the farthest?
PEDANT.   Sir, at the farthest for a week or two:
But then up farther, and as far as Rome;
And so to Tripoli, if God lend me life.
TRANIO.   What countryman, I pray?
PEDANT.   Of Mantua.
TRANIO.   Of Mantua, sir? marry, God forbid!
And come to Padua, careless of your life?
PEDANT.   My life, sir! how, I pray? for that goes hard.
TRANIO.   'Tis death for any one in Mantua
To come to Padua.   Know you not the cause?
Your ships are stay'd at Venice, and the duke,
For private quarrel 'twixt your duke and him,
Hath publish'd and proclaim'd it openly:
'Tis marvel, but that you are but newly come,
You might have heard it else proclaim'd about.
PEDANT.   Alas! sir, it is worse for me than so;
For I have bills for money by exchange
From Florence and must here deliver them.
TRANIO.   Well, sir, to do you courtesy,
This will I do, and this I will advise you:
First, tell me, have you ever been at Pisa?
PEDANT.   Ay, sir, in Pisa have I often been,
Pisa renowned for grave citizens.
TRANIO.   Among them know you one Vincentio?
PEDANT.   I know him not, but I have heard of him;
A merchant of incomparable wealth.
TRANIO.   He is my father, sir; and, sooth to say,
In countenance somewhat doth resemble you.
BIONDELLO [*aside[.   As much as an apple doth an oyster, and all
    one.
TRANIO.   To save your life in this extremity,
This favour will I do you for his sake;

[1] *Sees* BIONDELLO *coming.   Motion* BIANCA *and* LUCENTIO *over* R.

[2] PEDANT *comes to* C.

And think it not the worst of all your fortunes
That you are like to Sir Vincentio.
His name and credit shall you undertake,
And in my house you shall be friendly lodged:
Look that you take upon you as you should ;
You understand me, sir : so shall you stay
Till you have done your business in the city :
If this be courtesy, sir, accept of it.
  PEDANT. O sir, I do ; and will repute you ever
The patron of my life and liberty.
  TRANIO. Then go with me to make the matter good.
This, by the way, I let you understand ;
My father is here look'd for every day,
To pass assurance of a dower in marriage
'Twixt me and one Baptista's daughter here :
In all these circumstances I'll instruct you :
Go with me to clothe you as becomes you.
                [*Exeunt* R.[1]

T,averse No. 1 *drawn off, exposing full scene set as before for* PETRU-
  CHIO's *house. Table is laid for three.*

SCENE III

PETRUCHIO'S *house.*

Enter C. GRUMIO *and* KATHARINA.[2]

  GRUMIO. No, no, forsooth ; I dare not for my life.
  KATHARINA. The more my wrong, the more his spite appears :
What, did he marry me to famish me ?
Beggars, that come unto my father's door,
Upon entreaty have a present alms ;
If not, elsewhere they meet with charity :
But I, who never knew how to entreat,
Nor never needed that I should entreat,
Am starved for meat, giddy for lack of sleep,
With oaths kept waking and with brawling fed :
And that which spites me more than all these wants,
He does it under name of perfect love ;
As who should say, if I should sleep or eat,
'Twere deadly sickness or else present death.[3]
I prithee go and get me some repast ;
I care not what, so it be wholesome food.
  GRUMIO. What say you to a neat's foot ?[4]
  KATHARINA. 'Tis passing good : I prithee let me have it.
  GRUMIO. I fear it is too choleric a meat.[5]
How say you to a fat tripe finely broil'd ?[6]
  KATHARINA. I like it well : good Grumio, fetch it me.
  GRUMIO. I cannot tell ; I fear 'tis choleric.[7]
What say you to a piece of beef and mustard ?[8]
  KATHARINA. A dish that I do love to feed upon.
  GRUMIO. Ay, but the mustard is too hot a little.[9]
  KATHARINA. Why then, the beef, and let the mustard rest.
  GRUMIO. Nay then, I will not : you shall have the mustard,
Or else you get no beef of Grumio.

---

[1] TRANIO, PEDANT *together*, BIONDELLO *following.*

[2] GRUMIO *stands at entrance.* KATHARINA, *speaking as she moves, comes down* L. *Crosses front to* R., *then back and sinks in chair* L. *end of table.* GRUMIO *hovers at back.*

[3] GRUMIO *has moved down* L.

[4] *With a cheerful tone.*

[5] *Dashing her hopes.*

[6] *Again with great cheerfulness.*

[7] *Business for* KATHARINA *as at* [5]

[8] *More cheerful still.*

[9] *Same business for* KATHARINA.

KATHARINA.   Then both, or one, or anything thou wilt.
GRUMIO.   Why then, the mustard without the beef.
KATHARINA.[1]   Go, get thee gone, thou false deluding slave,
                                              [*Beats him.*
That feed'st me with the very name of meat:
Sorrow on thee and all the pack of you,
That triumph thus upon my misery!
Go, get thee gone, I say.

Enter PETRUCHIO *and* HORTENSIO *with meat* C.   KATHARINA *is* R.,
                    GRUMIO L.

PETRUCHIO.   How fares my Kate? What, sweeting, all amort?
HORTENSIO.   Mistress, what cheer?[2]
KATHARINA.   Faith, as cold as can be.
PETRUCHIO.   Pluck up thy spirits; look cheerfully upon me,
Here, love; thou see'st how diligent I am
To dress thy meat myself and bring it thee:
I am sure, sweet Kate, this kindness merits thanks.
What, not a word? Nay, then thou lovest it not:
And all my pains is sorted to no proof.
Here, take away this dish.
      KATHARINA.   I pray you, let it stand.
PETRUCHIO.   The poorest service is repaid with thanks;
And so shall mine, before you touch the meat.
      KATHARINA.   I thank you, sir.
HORTENSIO.   Signior Petruchio, fie! you are to blame.
Come, Mistress Kate, I'll bear you company.[3]
      PETRUCHIO[4] [*aside*].   Eat it up all, Hortensio, if thou lovest me.
Much good do it unto thy gentle heart!
[5]Kate, eat apace; and now, my honey love,[6]
Will we return unto thy father's house
And revel it as bravely as the best,[7]
With silken coats and caps and golden rings,
With ruffs and cuffs and fardingales and things;[8]
With scarfs and fans and double change of bravery,
With amber bracelets, beads and all this knavery.[9]
What, hast thou dined?[10] The tailor stays thy leisure,
To deck thy body with his ruffling treasure.

Enter TAILOR C.

[11] Come, tailor, let us see these ornaments;
Lay forth the gown.

Enter HABERDASHER C.

              What news with you, sir?
HABERDASHER.   Here is the cap your worship did bespeak.[12]
PETRUCHIO.   Why, this was moulded on a porringer;
A velvet dish: fie, fie! 'tis lewd and filthy:
Why, 'tis a cockle or a walnut-shell,
A knack, a toy, a trick, a baby's cap:
Away with it! come, let me have a bigger.[13]
      KATHARINA.[14]   I'll have no bigger: this doth fit the time,
And gentlewomen wear such caps as these.
PETRUCHIO.[15]   When you are gentle, you shall have one too,
And not till then.
      HORTENSIO [*aside*].   That will not be in haste.
D

[1] *Chasing him round table L. to R.*
KATHARINA is R, GRUMIO L.

[2] *HORTENSIO by chair L. of table. PETRU-*
CHIO C. at back.

[3] *They sit.* PETRUCHIO C. back, KATH-
ARINA R., HORTENSIO L., GRUMIO *by*
PETRUCHIO *stands serving drink.*
[4] PETRUCHIO *serves food, giving* HORTENSIO
a large portion.
[5] *Handing* KATHARINA *a minute portion.*
[6] *Helping himself to the rest.*

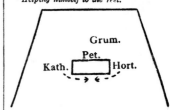

[7] *Drinks. As he drinks* HORTENSIO *passes*
KATHARINA *food on his fork below the*
level of the table top. She takes it off with
her fingers.
[8] *Repeat business of passing food.*
[9] PETRUCHIO *goes to drink again,* HORTENSIO
to pass food. PETRUCHIO *stops, leans,*
looks over table. HORTENSIO *passes fork*
to GRUMIO, *who passes it behind* PETRU-
CHIO'S *back to* KATHARINA.
[10] GRUMIO *motions that the* TAILOR *has*
arrived.
[11] KATHARINA *moves front L.* HORTENSIO
places his chair for her to sit on. PETRU-
CHIO *moves to C.* TAILOR R. HABER-
DASHER *enters during this movement to L.*
[12] *Handing cap to* PETRUCHIO.

[13] *Offering it back to* HABERDASHER.
[14] *Taking cap from* PETRUCHIO.

[15] *Taking cap from* KATHARINA.

KATHARINA. Why, sir, I trust I may have leave to speak;
And speak I will; I am no child, no babe:
Your betters have endured me say my mind,
And if you cannot, best you stop your ears.
My tongue will tell the anger of my heart,
Or else my heart concealing it will break,
And rather than it shall, I will be free
Even to the uttermost, as I please, in words.
PETRUCHIO. Why, thou say'st true; it is a paltry cap,
A custard coffin, a bauble, a silken pie:
I love thee well, in that thou likest it not.
KATHARINA. Love me or love me not, I like the cap;
And it I will have, or I will have none.[1]

[*Exit* HABERDASHER.

PETRUCHIO.[2] Thy gown? why, ay: come, tailor, let us see't.
O mercy, God! what masquing stuff is here?
What's this? a sleeve? 'tis like a demi-cannon:
What, up and down, carved like an apple-tart?
Here's snip and nip and cut and slish and slash,
Like to a censer in a barber's shop:
Why, what, i' devil's name, tailor, call'st thou this?
HORTENSIO [*aside*]. I see she's like to have neither cap nor gown.
TAILOR. You bid me make it orderly and well,
According to the fashion and the time.
PETRUCHIO. Marry, and did; but if you be remember'd,
I did not bid you mar it to the time.
Go, hop me over every kennel home.
For you shall hop without my custom, sir:
I'll none of it: hence! make your best of it.
KATHARINA. I never saw a better-fashion'd gown,
More quaint, more pleasing, nor more commendable:
Belike you mean to make a puppet of me.
PETRUCHIO. Why, true; he means to make a puppet of thee.
TAILOR. She says your worship means to make a puppet of her.
PETRUCHIO.[3] O monstrous arrogance! Thou liest, thou thread, thou thimble,
Thou yard, three-quarters, half-yard, quarter, nail!
Thou flea, thou nit, thou winter-cricket thou!
Braved in mine own house with a skein of thread?
Away, thou rag, thou quantity, thou remnant;
Or I shall so be-mete thee with thy yard
As thou shalt think on prating whilst thou livest!
I tell thee, I, that thou hast marr'd her gown.
TAILOR. Your worship is deceived; the gown is made
Just as my master had direction:
Grumio gave order how it should be done.[4]
GRUMIO. I gave him no order; I gave him the stuff.
TAILOR. But how did you desire it should be made?
GRUMIO. Marry, sir, with needle and thread.
TAILOR. But did you not request to have it cut?
GRUMIO.[5] Thou hast faced many things.
TAILOR. I have.
GRUMIO. Face not me: thou hast braved many men; brave not me; I will neither be faced nor braved. I say unto thee, I bid thy master cut out the gown; but I did not bid him cut it to pieces: *ergo*, thou liest.
TAILOR.[6] Why, here is the note of the fashion to testify.

[1] *Throws cap over to* HABERDASHER, *saying,* "*She will have none.*" HORTENSIO *takes* HABERDASHER *and dismisses him* O.

[2] *Taking gown.*

[3] *Advances on the* TAILOR *and backing him round to* L.

[4] PETRUCHIO *has backed* TAILOR *over to* GRUMIO; *he turns as* GRUMIO *speaks, so* TAILOR *and* GRUMIO *are facing one another.* PETRUCHIO *is sitting on table* O. *During* PETRUCHIO'S *attack on* TAILOR, HORTENSIO *has rescued* KATHARINA *and she is sitting by fire* L.

[5] *Pushing* TAILOR *to* O.

[6] *Falling to* R., GRUMIO *to* L.

PETRUCHIO. Read it.

GRUMIO. The note lies in's throat, if he say I said so.

TAILOR [reads]. *Imprimis, a loose-bodied gown* :

GRUMIO. Master, if ever I said loose-bodied gown, sew me in the skirts of it, and beat me to death with a bottom of brown thread : I said a gown.

PETRUCHIO. Proceed.

TAILOR [reads]. *With a small compassed cape* :

GRUMIO. I confess the cape.

TAILOR [reads]. *With a trunk sleeve* :

GRUMIO. I confess two sleeves.

TAILOR [reads]. *The sleeves curiously cut.*

PETRUCHIO. Ay, there's the villany.

GRUMIO. Error i' the bill, sir ; error i' the bill. I commanded the sleeves should be cut out and sewed up again ; and that I'll prove upon thee, though thy little finger be armed in a thimble.

TAILOR. This is true that I say ; an I had thee in place where thou shouldst know it.

GRUMIO. I am for thee straight ; take thou the bill, give me thy mete-yard, and spare not me.

HORTENSIO. God-a-mercy, Grumio ! then he shall have no odds.

PETRUCHIO. Well, sir, in brief, the gown is not for me.

GRUMIO. You are i' the right, sir : 'tis for my mistress.

PETRUCHIO. Go, take it up unto thy master's use.

GRUMIO. Villain, not for thy life : take up my mistress' gown for thy master's use !

PETRUCHIO. Why, sir, what's your conceit in that ?

GRUMIO. O, sir, the conceit is deeper than you think for :
Take up my mistress' gown to his master's use !
O, fie, fie, fie !

PETRUCHIO [aside]. Hortensio, say thou wilt see the tailor paid.
Go take it hence ; be gone, and say no more.

HORTENSIO.[1] Tailor, I'll pay thee for thy gown to-morrow :
Take no unkindness of his hasty words :
Away ! I say ; commend me to thy master.

[*Exit* TAILOR.

PETRUCHIO. Well, come, my Kate ; we will unto your father's
Even in these honest mean habiliments :
Our purses shall be proud, our garments poor ;
For 'tis the mind that makes the body rich ;
And as the sun breaks through the darkest clouds,
So honour peereth in the meanest habit.
What is the jay more precious than the lark
Because his feathers are more beautiful ?
Or is the adder better than the eel,
Because his painted skin contents the eye ?
O, no, good Kate ; neither art thou the worse
For this poor furniture and mean array.
If thou account'st it shame, lay it on me,
And therefore frolic ; we will hence forthwith,
To feast and sport us at thy father's house.
Go, call my men, and let us straight to him ;
And bring our horses unto Long-lane end ;
There will we mount, and thither walk on foot.
Let's see ; I think 'tis now some seven o'clock,
And well we may come there by dinner-time.

[1] *Crossing to* TAILOR, *takes him up* R. *to* C.
GRUMIO *moves up* L. *to back, comes back*
R. *with* HORTENSIO.

KATHARINA.¹ I dare assure you, sir, 'tis almost two;
And 'twill be supper-time ere you come there.
   PETRUCHIO. It shall be seven ere I go to horse:
Look, what I speak, or do, or think to do,
You are still crossing it. Sirs, let's alone:
I will not go to-day; and ere I do,
It shall be what o'clock I say it is.²
   HORTENSIO [*aside*]. Why, so this gallant will command the sun.
                                                      [*Exeunt.*

*Traverse No. 1 drawn over. Stage cleared. Traverse No. 2 drawn
          over. Traverse No. 1 drawn off.*

SCENE IV.

Padua. Before BAPTISTA'S *house.*

Enter TRANIO, *and the* PEDANT *dressed like* VINCENTIO. **L.**

   TRANIO. Sir, this is the house: please it you that I call?³
   PEDANT. Ay, what else? and but I be deceived
Signior Baptista may remember me,
Near twenty years ago, in Genoa,
Where we were lodgers at the Pegasus.
   TRANIO. 'Tis well; and hold your own, in any case,
With such austerity as 'longeth to a father.
   PEDANT. I warrant you.

                 Enter BIONDELLO **L.**

                        But, sir, here comes your boy;
'Twere good he were school'd.
   TRANIO. Fear you not him. Sirrah Biondello,
Now do your duty thoroughly, I advise you:
Imagine 'twere the right Vincentio.
   BIONDELLO. Tut, fear not me.
   TRANIO. But hast thou done thy errand to Baptista?
   BIONDELLO. I told him that your father was at Venice,
And that you look'd for him this day in Padua.
   TRANIO. Thou'rt a tall fellow: hold thee that to drink.
Here comes Baptista: set your countenance, sir.

           Enter BAPTISTA *and* LUCENTIO **L.**

Signior Baptista, you are happily met.
[*To the* PEDANT.] Sir, this is the gentleman I told you of:
I pray you, stand good father to me now,
Give me Bianca for my patrimony.
   PEDANT. Soft, son!⁴

Sir, by your leave: having come to Padua
To gather in some debts, my son Lucentio
Made me acquainted with a weighty cause
Of love between your daughter and himself:
And, for the good report I hear of you
And for the love he beareth to your daughter
And she to him, to stay him not too long,
I am content, in a good father's care,
To have him match'd; and if you please to like

No worse than I, upon some agreement
Me shall you find ready and willing
With one consent to have her so bestow'd ;
For curious I cannot be with you,
Signior Baptista, of whom I hear so well.

BAPTISTA. Sir, pardon me in what I have to say :
Your plainness and your shortness please me well.
Right true it is, your son Lucentio here
Doth love my daughter and she loveth him,
Or both dissemble deeply their affections :
And therefore, if you say no more than this,
That like a father you will deal with him
And pass my daughter a sufficient dower,
The match is made, and all is done :
Your son shall have my daughter with consent.

TRANIO.[1] I thank you, sir. Where then do you know best
We be affied and such assurance ta'en
As shall with either part's agreement stand ?

BAPTISTA. Not in my house, Lucentio ; for, you know,
Pitchers have ears, and I have many servants :
Besides, old Gremio is hearkening still ;
And happily we might be interrupted.

TRANIO. Then at my lodging, an it like you :
There doth my father lie ; and there, this night,
We'll pass the business privately and well.
Send for your daughter by your servant here ;
My boy shall fetch the scrivener presently.
The worst is this, that, at so slender warning,
You are like to have a thin and slender pittance.

BAPTISTA. It likes me well. Cambio, hie you home,
And bid Bianca make her ready straight ;
And, if you will, tell what hath happened,
Lucentio's father is arrived in Padua,
And how she's like to be Lucentio's wife.

LUCENTIO. I pray the gods she may with all my heart !

TRANIO. Dally not with the gods, but get thee gone.

[*Exit* LUCENTIO R.

Signior Baptista, shall I lead the way ?
Welcome ! one mess is like to be your cheer :
Come, sir ; we will better it in Pisa.

BAPTISTA. I follow you.

[*Exeunt* TRANIO, PEDANT, *and* BAPTISTA L.[2]

BIONDELLO.[3] Cambio !

Re-enter LUCENTIO.

LUCENTIO. What sayest thou, Biondello ?

BIONDELLO. You saw my master wink and laugh upon you ?

LUCENTIO. Biondello, what of that ?

BIONDELLO. Faith, nothing : but has left me here behind, to
expound the meaning or moral of his signs and tokens.

LUCENTIO. I pray thee, moralize them.

BIONDELLO. Then thus. Baptista is safe, talking with the deceiv-
ing father of a deceitful son.

LUCENTIO. And what of him ?

BIONDELLO. His daughter is to be brought by you to the supper.

LUCENTIO. And then ?

[1] *Crossing to* BAPTISTA. PEDANT *crosses round at back to* BIONDELLO.

[2] *Ceremonially bowing one to the other.*
[3] *Crossing to door* R.

BIONDELLO. The old priest of Saint Luke's church is at your command at all hours.

LUCENTIO. And what of all this ?

BIONDELLO. I cannot tell ; expect they are busied about a counterfeit assurance : take you assurance of her, *cum privilegio ad imprimendum solum* : to the church ; take the priest, clerk, and some sufficient honest witnesses :
If this be not that you look for, I have no more to say,
But bid Bianca farewell for ever and a day.

LUCENTIO. Hearest thou, Biondello ?

BIONDELLO. I cannot tarry : I knew a wench married in an afternoon as she went to the garden for parsley to stuff a rabbit ; and so may you, sir ; and so, adieu, sir. My master hath appointed me to go to Saint Luke's, to bid the priest be ready to come against you come with your appendix.   [*Exit* L.

LUCENTIO. I may, and will, if she be so contented :
She will be pleased ; then wherefore should I doubt ?
Hap what hap may, I'll roundly go about her :
It shall go hard if Cambio go without her.   [*Exit* R.[1]

SCENE V

A public place.

Enter PETRUCHIO, KATHARINA, HORTENSIO *and* GRUMIO L.[2]

PETRUCHIO.[3] Come on, i' God's name ; once more toward our father's.
Good Lord, how bright and goodly shines the moon !

KATHARINA. The moon ! the sun : it is not moonlight now.

PETRUCHIO. I say it is the moon that shines so bright.

KATHARINA. I know it is the sun that shines so bright.

PETRUCHIO. Now, by my mother's son, and that's myself,
It shall be moon, or star, or what I list,
Or ere I journey to your father's house.
Go on, and fetch our horses back again.
Evermore cross'd and cross'd ; nothing but cross'd ! [4]

HORTENSIO.[5] Say as he says, or we shall never go.

KATHARINA. Forward, I pray, since we have come so far,
And be it moon, or sun, or what you please :
An if you please to call it a rush-candle,
Henceforth I vow it shall be so for me.

PETRUCHIO. I say it is the moon.

KATHARINA.   I know it is the moon.

PETRUCHIO. Nay, then you lie : it is the blessed sun.

KATHARINA. Then, God be bless'd, it is the blessed sun :
But sun it is not, when you say it is not ;
And the moon changes even as your mind.
What you will have it named, even that it is ;
And so it shall be so for Katharine.[6]

HORTENSIO.[7] Petruchio, go thy ways ; the field is won.

PETRUCHIO. Well, forward, forward ! thus the bowl should run,
And not unluckily against the bias.
But, soft ! company is coming here.[8]

Enter VINCENTIO R.[9]

[Left margin notes:]

[1] *When stage is clear* PLAYERS' BOY *enters from down* R. *and exhibits Location Card " A Public Place." He retires same entrance. Traverse 2 remains.*

[2] *In the order named.*

[3] PETRUCHIO *crosses to* R., KATHARINA *stops at* C., HORTENSIO *and* GRUMIO L.

[4] PETRUCHIO *to extreme* R.

[5] *Advancing to* KATHARINA *as* PETRUCHIO *walks* R.

[6] KATHARINA *a step to* L.

[7] *Advances to* PETRUCHIO.

[8] *As about to go* R.

[9] *Crossing in front of* PETRUCHIO *and* HORTENSIO *towards* KATHARINA C.

[*To* VINCENTIO]   Good morrow, gentle mistress: where away ?
Tell me, sweet Kate, and tell me truly too,
Hast thou beheld a fresher gentlewoman ?
Such war of white and red within her cheeks !
What stars do spangle heaven with such beauty,
As those two eyes become that heavenly face ?
Fair lovely maid, once more good day to thee.
Sweet Kate, embrace her for her beauty's sake.

    HORTENSIO.   A will make the man mad, to make a woman of him.

    KATHARINA.[1]   Young budding virgin, fair and fresh and sweet,
Whither away, or where is thy abode ?
Happy the parents of so fair a child ;
Happier the man, whom favourable stars
Allot thee for his lovely bed-fellow !

    PETRUCHIO.[2]   Why, how now, Kate ! I hope thou art not mad :
This is a man, old, wrinkled, faded, wither'd,
And not a maiden, as thou say'st he is.

    KATHARINA.   Pardon, old father, my mistaking eyes,
That have been so bedazzled with the [3] sun
That everything I look on seemeth [4] green : [5]
Now I perceive thou art a reverend father ;
Pardon, I pray thee, for my mad mistaking.

    PETRUCHIO.   Do, good old grandsire ; and withal make known
Which way thou travellest : if along with us,
We shall be joyful of thy company.

    VINCENTIO.   Fair sir, and you my merry mistress,
That with your strange encounter much amazed me,
My name is call'd Vincentio ; my dwelling Pisa ;
And bound I am to Padua ; there to visit
A son of mine, which long I have not seen.

    PETRUCHIO.   What is his name ?

    VINCENTIO.   Lucentio, gentle sir.

    PETRUCHIO.   Happily met ; the happier for thy son.
And now by law, as well as reverend age,
I may entitle thee my loving father :
The sister to my wife, this gentlewoman,
Thy son by this hath married. Wonder not,
Nor be not grieved : she is of good esteem,
Her dowry wealthy, and of worthy birth ;
Beside, so qualified as may beseem
The spouse of any noble gentleman.
[6] Let me embrace with old Vincentio,
And wander we to see thy honest son,
Who will of thy arrival be full joyous.

    VINCENTIO.   But is this true ? or is it else your pleasure,
Like pleasant travellers, to break a jest
Upon the company you overtake ?

    HORTENSIO.   I do assure thee, father, so it is.

    PETRUCHIO.   Come, go along, and see the truth hereof ;
For our first merriment hath made thee jealous.

                     [*Exeunt all but* HORTENSIO R.[7]

    HORTENSIO.   Well, Petruchio, this has put me in heart.
Have to my widow ! and if she be froward,
Then hast thou taught Hortensio to be untoward.

                           [*Exit* R.

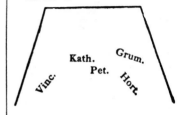

[1] *Traverse 2 remains.* PLAYERS' BOY *enters from* R. *down stage with Location Card,* "*Before Lucentio's Lodging.*"

[2] *He runs to door* R. *and knocks.*

[3] *Up stage.*

[4] *Down stage.*

[5] *Crosses to* R. *up stage.*

[6] PETRUCHIO *first,* VINCENTIO *and* KATHARINA *second,* GRUMIO *third.*

[7] *Crossing to door.* PETRUCHIO *to* KATHARINA L.

[8] *Coming at back to* L.C., *he greets* PETRUCHIO *and* KATHARINA L.

[9] *Balcony* R.

[10] *Coming to* C. *down stage.*

SCENE VI.[1]

Padua.   Before LUCENTIO'S *lodging.*

Enter BIONDELLO L.[2]

Enter LUCENTIO *and* BIANCA *door* R.

BIONDELLO.   Softly and swiftly, sir ; for the priest is ready.

LUCENTIO.   I fly, Biondello : but they may chance to need thee at home ; therefore leave us.

BIONDELLO.   Nay, faith, I'll see the church o' your back ; and then come back to my master's as soon as I can.

[*Exeunt* LUCENTIO, BIANCA *and* BIONDELLO L.[3]

Enter GREMIO L.[4]

GREMIO.   I marvel Cambio comes not all this while.[5]

Enter PETRUCHIO, KATHARINA, VINCENTIO *and* GRUMIO L.[6]

PETRUCHIO.   Sir, here's the door, this is Lucentio's house : My father's bears more toward the market-place ; Thither must I, and here I leave you, sir.

VINCENTIO.   You shall not choose but drink before you go : I think I shall command your welcome here,[7] And, by all likelihood, some cheer is toward.

[*Knocks.*

GREMIO.[8]   They're busy within ; you were best knock louder.

PEDANT *looks out of the window.*[9]

PEDANT.   What's he that knocks as he would beat down the gate ?

VINCENTIO.   Is Signior Lucentio within, sir ?

PEDANT.   He's within, sir, but not to be spoken withal.

VINCENTIO.   What if a man bring him a hundred pound or two, to make merry withal ?

PEDANT.   Keep your hundred pounds to yourself : he shall need none, so long as I live.

PETRUCHIO.[10]   Nay, I told you your son was well beloved in Padua. Do you hear, sir ?   To leave frivolous circumstances, I pray you, tell Signior Lucentio that his father is come from Pisa and is here at the door to speak with him.

PEDANT.   Thou liest : his father is come from Padua and here looking out at the window.

VINCENTIO.   Art thou his father ?

PEDANT.   Ay, sir ; so his mother says, if I may believe her.

PETRUCHIO [*to* VINCENTIO].   Why, how now, gentleman ! why, this is flat knavery, to take upon you another man's name.

PEDANT.   Lay hands on the villain : I believe a' means to cozen somebody in this city under my countenance.

Re-enter BIONDELLO.

BIONDELLO. I have seen them in the church together: God send 'em good shipping! But who is here? mine old master Vincentio! now we are undone and brought to nothing.[1]

VINCENTIO [*seeing* BIONDELLO]. Come hither, crack-hemp.[2]

BIONDELLO. I hope I may choose, sir.[3]

VINCENTIO. Come hither, you rogue.[4] What, have you forgot me?

BIONDELLO. Forgot you! no, sir: I could not forget you, for I never saw you before in all my life.

VINCENTIO. What, you notorious villain, didst thou never see thy master's father, Vincentio?

BIONDELLO.[5] What, my old worshipful old master? yes, marry, sir: see where he looks out of the window.

VINCENTIO. Is't so, indeed?

[*Beats* BIONDELLO *round stage.*

BIONDELLO.[6] Help, help, help! here's a madman will murder me.

[*Exit.*

PEDANT. Help, son! help, Signior Baptista!

[*Exit from above.*

PETRUCHIO. Prithee, Kate, let's stand aside and see the end of this controversy.

[PETRUCHIO *and* KATHARINA *retire down* L.

Enter from door R., TRANIO, BAPTISTA *and* PEDANT, *followed by* SERVANTS.

TRANIO. Sir, what are you that offer to beat my servant?

VINCENTIO. What am I, sir! nay, what are you, sir? O immortal gods! O fine villain! A silken doublet! a velvet hose! a scarlet cloak! and a copatain hat! O, I am undone! I am undone! while I play the good husband at home, my son and my servant spend all at the university.

TRANIO. How now! what's the matter?

BAPTISTA. What, is the man lunatic?

TRANIO. Sir, you seem a sober ancient gentleman by your habit, but your words show you a madman. Why, sir, what 'cerns it you if I wear pearl and gold? I thank my good father, I am able to maintain it.

VINCENTIO. Thy father! O villain! he is a sail-maker in Bergamo.

BAPTISTA.[7] You mistake, sir, you mistake, sir. Pray, what do you think is his name?

VINCENTIO. His name! as if I knew not his name: I have brought him up ever since he was three years old, and his name is Tranio.

PEDANT. Away, away, mad ass! his name is Lucentio: and he is mine only son, and heir to the lands of me, Signior Vincentio.[8]

VINCENTIO. Lucentio! O, he hath murdered his master! Lay hold on him, I charge you, in the duke's name. O, my son, my son! Tell me, thou villain, where is my son Lucentio?

TRANIO. Call forth an officer. Carry this mad knave to the gaol. Father Baptista, I charge you see that he be forthcoming.

VINCENTIO. Carry me to the gaol!

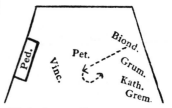

[1] *Begins to creep off.*
[2] BIONDELLO *stops.*
[3] *Turning to go again.*
[4] BIONDELLO *stops, turning to* VINCENTIO.

[5] *Coming* O.

[6] BIONDELLO *runs round behind* PETRUCHIO *in a circle, followed by* VINCENTIO *and off* L. *At conclusion of this business* VINCENTIO *remains up stage* R.O.

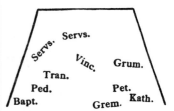

[7] *Going up to* VINCENTIO O. *in front of* PEDANT *and* TRANIO.

[8] *Getting a little up stage behind* TRANIO.

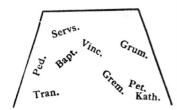

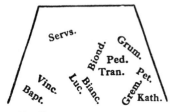

GREMIO. Stay: he shall not go to prison.

BAPTISTA Talk not, Signior Gremio: I say he shall go to prison.

GREMIO. Take heed, Signior Baptista, lest you be cony-catched in this business: I dare swear this is the right Vincentio.

PEDANT. Swear, if thou darest.[1]

GREMIO. Nay, I dare not swear it.[2]

TRANIO.[3] Then thou wert best say that I am not Lucentio.

GREMIO. Yes, I know thee to be Signior Lucentio.[4]

BAPTISTA. Away with the dotard! to the gaol with him!

VINCENTIO.[5] Thus strangers may be haled and abused: O monstrous villain!

Re-enter BIONDELLO, *with* LUCENTIO *and* BIANCA L. *up stage.*

BIONDELLO. O! we are spoiled and—yonder he is: deny him, forswear him, or else we are all undone.

LUCENTIO [*kneeling*]. Pardon, sweet father.

VINCENTIO. Lives my sweet son?[6]

[*Exeunt* BIONDELLO, TRANIO *and* PEDANT *as fast as may be.*[7]

BIANCA. Pardon, dear father.

BAPTISTA. How hast thou offended? Where is Lucentio?

LUCENTIO. Here's Lucentio,
Right son to the right Vincentio;
That have by marriage made thy daughter mine,
While counterfeit supposes blear'd thine eyne.

GREMIO. Here's packing, with a witness, to deceive us all!

VINCENTIO. Where is that damned villain Tranio,
That faced and braved me in this matter so?

BAPTISTA. Why, tell me, is not this my Cambio?

BIANCA. Cambio is changed into Lucentio.

LUCENTIO. Love wrought these miracles. Bianca's love
Made me exchange my state with Tranio,
While he did bear my countenance in the town;
And happily I have arrived at the last
Unto the wished haven of my bliss.
What Tranio did, myself enforced him to;
Then pardon him, sweet father, for my sake.

VINCENTIO. I'll slit the villain's nose, that would have sent me to the gaol.

BAPTISTA. But do you hear, sir? have you married my daughter without asking my good will?

VINCENTIO. Fear not, Baptista; we will content you, go to: but I will in, to be revenged for this villany. [*Exit door* R.

BAPTISTA. And I, to sound the depth of this knavery.
[*Exit door* R.

LUCENTIO. Look not pale, Bianca; thy father will not frown.
[*Exeunt* LUCENTIO *and* BIANCA R.

GREMIO.[8] My cake is dough; but I'll in among the rest,
Out of hope of all, but my share of the feast.
[*Exit* R.[9]

KATHARINA.[10] Husband, let's follow, to see the end of this ado.

PETRUCHIO. First kiss me, Kate, and we will.

KATHARINA. What, in the midst of the street?

PETRUCHIO. What, art thou ashamed of me?

KATHARINA. No, sir, God forbid; but ashamed to kiss.

PETRUCHIO. Why, then let's home again.[11] Come, sirrah, let's away.

KATHARINA.   Nay, I will give thee a kiss;[1] now pray thee, love,
stay.
PETRUCHIO.   Is not this well ? Come, my sweet Kate:
Better once than never, for never too late.
[Exeunt R., followed by GRUMIO.

Traverse I is drawn over.

[1] Kissing him.

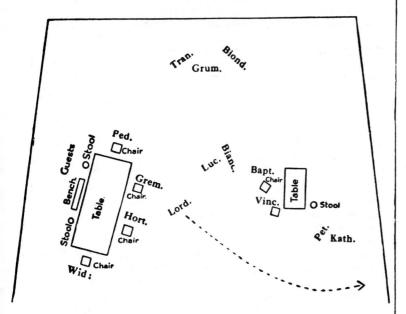

SCENE VII

Padua. LUCENTIO'S house.[2]

BAPTISTA, VINCENTIO, PETRUCHIO, KATHARINA, BIANCA, LUCENTIO,
GRUMIO, TRANIO, BIONDELLO, PEDANT, GREMIO, HORTENSIO,
WIDOW, GUESTS and the LORD are discovered.

LUCENTIO.   At last, though long, our jarring notes agree:
And time it is, when raging war is done,
To smile at scapes and perils overblown.
My fair Bianca, bid my father welcome,
While I with self-same kindness welcome thine.
Brother Petruchio, sister Katharine,
And thou, Hortensio, with thy loving widow,
Feast with the best, and welcome to my house:
My banquet is to close our stomachs up,
After our great good cheer. Pray you, sit down;
For now we sit to chat as well as eat.
PETRUCHIO.   Nothing but sit and sit, and eat and eat!
BAPTISTA.   Padua affords this kindness, son Petruchio.
PETRUCHIO.   Padua affords nothing but what is kind.
HORTENSIO.   For both our sakes, I would that word were true.
PETRUCHIO.[3]   Now, for my life, Hortensio fears his widow.
WIDOW.   Then never trust me, if I be afeard.
PETRUCHIO.   You are very sensible, and yet you miss my sense:
I mean, Hortensio is afeard of you.

[2] Full stage. Furniture to be quickly set.
Traverse 1 to be drawn off. Fruit, wine,
etc., on tables R. and L. The LORD is
discovered talking amongst the players;
after a moment he crosses the stage to his
seat L. All the Players should be standing.
They sit (those who are by their chairs) as
the LORD sits.

[3] Crossing to HORTENSIO. BIANCA and
LUCENTIO cross to KATHARINA.

¹ *Coming O.*

WIDOW. He that is giddy thinks the world turns round.
PETRUCHIO. Roundly replied.
KATHARINA.   Mistress, how mean you that? [1]
WIDOW. Thus I conceive by him.
PETRUCHIO. Conceives by me! How likes Hortensio that?
HORTENSIO. My widow says, thus she conceives her tale.
PETRUCHIO. Very well mended. Kiss him for that, good widow.
KATHARINA. *He that is giddy thinks the world turns round*
I pray you, tell me what you meant by that.
WIDOW. Your husband, being troubled with a shrew,
Measures my husband's sorrow by his woe:
And now you know my meaning.
KATHARINA. A very mean meaning.
WIDOW.   Right, I mean you.
KATHARINA. And I am mean indeed, respecting you.
PETRUCHIO. To her, Kate!
HORTENSIO. To her, widow!
PETRUCHIO. A hundred marks, my Kate does put her down.
HORTENSIO. That's my office.
PETRUCHIO. Spoke like an officer: ha' to thee, lad!

[*Drinks to* HORTENSIO. [2]

² PETRUCHIO *and* KATHARINA *move to back.*

³ *Crossing to* GREMIO.

BAPTISTA. [3] How likes Gremio these quick-witted folks?
GREMIO. Believe me, sir, they butt together well.
BIANCA. Head, and butt! an hasty-witted body
Would say your head and butt were head and horn.
VINCENTIO. Ay, mistress bride, hath that awaken'd you?
BIANCA. Ay, but not frighted me; therefore I'll sleep again.
PETRUCHIO. [4] Nay, that you shall not: since you have begun,
Have at you for a bitter jest or two!
BIANCA. [5] Am I your bird? I mean to shift my bush;
And then pursue me as you draw your bow.
You are welcome all.

⁴ *Coming down to* BIANCA L.

⁵ *Wheeling to O.*

[*Exeunt* BIANCA, KATHARINA *and* WIDOW *and lady guests* C.

PETRUCHIO. [6] She hath prevented me. Here, Signior Tranio,
This bird you aim'd at, though you hit her not;
Therefore a health to all that shot and miss'd.
TRANIO. O, sir, Lucentio slipp'd me like his grey-hound,
Which runs himself and catches for his master.
PETRUCHIO. A good swift simile, but something currish.
TRANIO. 'Tis well, sir, that you hunted for yourself:
'Tis thought your deer does hold you at a bay.
BAPTISTA. O ho, Petruchio! Tranio hits you now.
LUCENTIO. I thank thee for that gird, good Tranio.
HORTENSIO. Confess, confess, hath he not hit you here?
PETRUCHIO. A' has a little gall'd me, I confess;
And, as the jest did glance away from me,
'Tis ten to one it maim'd you two outright. [7]
BAPTISTA. Now, in good sadness, son Petruchio,
I think thou hast the veriest shrew of all.
PETRUCHIO. Well, I say no: and therefore for assurance
Let's each one send unto his wife;
And he whose wife is most obedient
To come at first when he doth send for her,
Shall win the wager which we will propose.
HORTENSIO. Content. What is the wager?
LUCENTIO.

                                 Twenty crowns.

⁶ PETRUCHIO *to table* R. HORTENSIO *moves to* WIDOW'S *seat.* BAPTISTA *moves over to* VINCENTIO, *then sits* L. *of small table.*

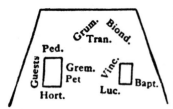

⁷ *Sits. Turning chair below* GREMIO, *out from table.*

PETRUCHIO.   Twenty crowns !
I'll venture so much of my hawk or hound,
But twenty times so much upon my wife.
   LUCENTIO.   A hundred then.
   HORTENSIO.   Content.
   PETRUCHIO.   A match ! 'tis done.
   HORTENSIO.   Who shall begin ?
   LUCENTIO.   That will I.
Go, Biondello, bid your mistress come to me.
   BIONDELLO.   I go.   [*Exit* C.
   BAPTISTA.   Son, I'll be your half, Bianca comes.
   LUCENTIO.   I'll have no halves ; I'll bear it all myself.

Re-enter BIONDELLO.

How now ! what news ?
   BIONDELLO.   Sir, my mistress sends you word
That she is busy and she cannot come.
   PETRUCHIO.   How ! she is busy and she cannot come
Is that an answer ?
   GREMIO.   Ay, and a kind one too :
Pray God, sir, your wife send you not a worse.
   PETRUCHIO.   I hope, better.
   HORTENSIO.   Sirrah Biondello, go and entreat my wife
To come to me forthwith.
                  [*Exit* BIONDELLO.

   PETRUCHIO.   O, ho ! entreat her !
Nay, then she must needs come.
   HORTENSIO.   I am afraid, sir,
Do what you can, yours will not be entreated.

Re-enter BIONDELLO.

Now, where's my wife ?
   BIONDELLO.   She says you have some goodly jest in hand :
She will not come ; she bids you come to her.
   PETRUCHIO.   Worse and worse ; she will not come ! O vile,
Intolerable, not to be endured !
Sirrah Grumio, go to your mistress ;
Say, I command her come to me.[1]
                [*Exit* GRUMIO.
   HORTENSIO.   I know her answer.
   PETRUCHIO.   What ?
   HORTENSIO.   She will not.
   PETRUCHIO.   The fouler fortune mine, and there an end.
   BAPTISTA.   Now, by my holidame, here comes Katharina !

Re-enter KATHARINA.

   KATHARINA.   What is your will, sir, that you send for me ?
   PETRUCHIO.   Where is your sister, and Hortensio's wife ?
   KATHARINA.   They sit conferring by the parlour fire.
   PETRUCHIO.   Go, fetch them hither : if they deny to come,
Swinge me them soundly forth unto their husbands :
Away, I say, and bring them hither straight.
               [*Exit* KATHARINA.
   LUCENTIO.   Here is a wonder, if you talk of a wonder.

[1] *Assuming an easy attitude and stretching his legs.*

HORTENSIO. And so it is: I wonder what it bodes.

PETRUCHIO. Marry, peace it bodes, and love and quiet life,
An awful rule and right supremacy;
And, to be short, what not, that's sweet and happy.

BAPTISTA. Now, fair befal thee, good Petruchio!
The wager thou hast won; and I will add
Unto their losses twenty thousand crowns;
Another dowry to another daughter,
For she is changed, as she had never been.

PETRUCHIO. Nay, I will win my wager better yet
And show more sign of her obedience,
Her new-built virtue and obedience.
See where she comes and brings your froward wives [1]
As prisoners to her womanly persuasion.

Re-enter KATHARINA, *with* BIANCA *and* WIDOW C.[2]

Katharine, that cap of yours becomes you not:
Off with that bauble, throw it under-foot.[3]

WIDOW. Lord, let me never have a cause to sigh,
Till I be brought to such a silly pass!

BIANCA. Fie! what a foolish duty call you this?

LUCENTIO. I would your duty were as foolish too:
The wisdom of your duty, fair Bianca.
Hath cost me an hundred crowns since supper-time.

BIANCA. The more fool you, for laying on my duty.

PETRUCHIO. Katharina, I charge thee, tell these headstrong women
What duty they do owe their lords and husbands.

WIDOW. Come, come, you're mocking: we will have no telling.

PETRUCHIO. Come on, I say; and first begin with her.

WIDOW. She shall not.

PETRUCHIO. I say she shall; and first begin with her.

KATHARINA. Fie, fie! unknit that threatening unkind brow,
And dart not scornful glances from those eyes,
To wound thy lord, thy king, thy governor:
It blots thy beauty as frosts do bite the meads,
Confounds thy fame as whirlwinds shake fair buds,
And in no sense is meet or amiable.
A woman moved is like a fountain troubled,
Muddy, ill-seeming, thick, bereft of beauty;
And while it is so, none so dry or thirsty
Will deign to sip or touch one drop of it.
Thy husband is thy lord, thy life, thy keeper,
Thy head, thy sovereign; one that cares for thee,
And for thy maintenance commits his body
To painful labour both by sea and land,
To watch the night in storms, the day in cold,
Whilst thou liest warm at home, secure and safe;
And craves no other tribute at thy hands
But love, fair looks and true obedience;
Too little payment for so great a debt.
Such duty as the subject owes the prince
Even such a woman oweth to her husband;
And when she is froward, peevish, sullen, sour,
And not obedient to his honest will,
What is she but a foul contending rebel

[margin notes:]

¹ *Rises.*

² *All who are seated rise as* KATHARINA *enters.* KATHARINA *throws* BIANCA *to* LUCENTIO L., *the* WIDOW *to* HORTENSIO R.

³ KATHARINA *removes cap.*

And graceless traitor to her loving lord ?
I am ashamed that women are so simple
To offer war where they should kneel for peace,
Or seek for rule, supremacy and sway,
When they are bound to serve, love and obey.
Why are our bodies soft and weak and smooth,
Unapt to toil and trouble in the world,
But that our soft conditions and our hearts
Should well agree with our external parts ?
Come, come, you froward and unable worms !
My mind hath been as big as one of yours,
My heart as great, my reason haply more,
To bandy word for word and frown for frown ;
But now I see our lances are but straws,
Our strength as weak, our weakness past compare,
That seeming to be most which we indeed least are.
Then vail your stomach, for it is no boot,
And place your hands below your husband's foot :
In token of which duty, if he please,
My hand is ready : may it do him ease.
   PETRUCHIO. Why, there's a wench ! Come on, and kiss me,
Kate.
   LUCENTIO. Well, go thy ways, old lad ; for thou shalt ha't.
   VINCENTIO. 'Tis a good hearing when children are toward.
   LUCENTIO. But a harsh hearing when women are froward.
   PETRUCHIO. Come, Kate, we'll to bed.
We three are married, but you two are sped.
[*To* LUCENTIO]. 'Twas I won the wager, though you hit the white ;
And, being a winner, God give you good night !
            [*Exeunt* PETRUCHIO *and* KATHARINA C.
   HORTENSIO. Now, go thy ways ; thou hast tamed a curst shrew.
   LUCENTIO. 'Tis a wonder, by your leave, she will be tamed so.

The Company turn and bow to the LORD. *He advances to them to*
congratulate them. As he is doing so, two ATTENDANTS *carry* SLY
on from door R. *in his old attire. The Company laugh. When* C.
the attendants swing SLY *to and fro three times and pitch him clear*
of Traverse No. I, *which is at once drawn over leaving him huddled*
on the floor.

SCENE VIII.—EPILOGUE

The HOSTESS *enters* L.

NOTE.—The old anonymous play " The Taming of a Shrew " con-
cluded as follows ; and it seems highly probable that Shakespeare's
Comedy had some corresponding conclusion, which has not been
preserved.

   HOSTESS. Now that the darksome day is overpast,
And dawn appeareth in a crystal sky,
Now must I haste abroad. But soft, who is this ?
What ! Sly ! Oh ! wondrous hath he layne here all night.
I'll wake him, I think he's starved by this,
But that his belly was so stuft with ale.
What ! how Sly, awake for shame.
   SLY. S-s-some more wine. Whats all the Players gone ? Am
not I a Lord ?
   HOSTESS. A lord with a mission Come art thou drunken still ?
   SLY. Who's this ? Hostess ! Oh Lord, I have had

The bravest dream to-night that ever thou
Hadst in all thy life.

HOSTESS. I, marry, but you had best get you home,
For your wife will curse you for dreaming here to-night.

SLY. Will she? I know now how to tame a shrew,
I dreamt upon it all this night till now.
And thou hast waked me out of the best dream
That ever I had in my life, but I'll to my
Wife presently and tame her too, and if she anger me.

HOSTESS. Nay, tarry, Sly, for I'll go home with thee
And hear the rest that thou hast dreamt to-night.

[*Exit.*

THE TAMING OF THE SHREW

COMMENTARY

PART I SCENE I (Induction)

The nature of this play begins to assert itself at once in this opening scene. Liveliness, ingenuity of idea, spiritedness of action express themselves in the text, and must do so in the action. We know that we are beginning a robust comedy by the opening incident between SLY and the HOSTESS. Here is a piece of eccentric, abnormal and genuinely humorous characterization in the person of the drunken tinker that offers the substance out of which the entertaining value of the two scenes of the Induction are made. SLY is very clearly drawn and so obvious that further comment is unnecessary.

The opening scene between the LORD and the HUNTSMEN must be played with all the enthusiasm of youthful sportsmen, keen about the hounds and their comparative qualities and behaviour. All this comes to a sudden stop as the LORD discovers SLY snoring in his drunken sleep ; but the treatment must be as vigorous in its own way as that applied to the preceding passage. It is not, of course, of a joyous kind, but it must sustain the activity of the scene otherwise we shall get a sudden slump in the action, which besides dropping the interest, will make it difficult to pick it up again. The LORD is suddenly confronted with a most curious object which for a moment puzzles him, and then awakens his deep disgust.

" *Sirs, I will practise on this drunken man.*" Here we begin a new phase. The LORD is suddenly struck with a remarkable idea which he announces with measured-out emphasis, and then proceeds to elaborate with details carefully and fully stated with slight, separative pauses to enable each to have their effect.

In the long speech which follows, take a quicker pace, but make each of the ideas spontaneous. Don't deliver them as though they had been learnt by heart, but keep the life assertive by inventing as he goes along, and give to each invention its individual colour by using the words as leaders to the treatment. Imitate the servants in their method of addressing SLY and by these means make the speech picturesque and full of movement.

The LORD's welcome to the PLAYERS is a further means of sustaining the preceding action by a change of method. The arrival of the PLAYERS develops another idea in the LORD's imagination. His welcome is an immediate greeting both to them and to the new suggestion that they offer with their arrival and is not confined to polite greeting. It is broad with the new fact in his mind, and this fact lives in the ensuing address to the PLAYER, not of course with the breadth of the initial greeting offered to the new arrivals, but alert with exploitation. Unless this is present in some way, the scene will drop, however charming the LORD may be in his behaviour.

He then tells the PLAYER, remembered so well for a previous piece of acting, that he has come in a ' happy time '. Don't throw this away. It must not be exaggerated, but at the same time it must be lifted sufficiently to indicate the situation. Likewise, measure out, " *There is a lord will hear you play tonight* ". It introduces the purpose for which he wants them and also enables him to nurse his own private joke to himself. It also is an opportunity to vary the treatment a little.

The final instructions to the SERVANT about the part the PAGE is to play begin with careful precision, getting a little quicker in pace after the opening two lines, but never losing the necessary attentiveness to facts, without which the speech will be an anti-climax.

All these qualities of treatment will awaken the scene to its true nature and give it an impetus of lively movement. Use the words to their full advantage and so avoid the danger of adopting pace alone in mistake for action. The life is always in the words.

GLOSSARY OF WORDS

(The figures after each word or phrase in the glossary refer to the page and line numbers in the text.)

1. **Pheeze.** 1,1. ' I'll pheeze you '. Pay you out. It is an obsolete form of *feeze*; OE. *fysian* to drive. It came to mean ' to drive away, to put to flight, to frighten '.
2. **Stocks.** 1,2. The form of punishment by means of which the culprit sat on a bench with his feet protruding through two holes in front of him.
3. **Baggage.** 1,3. A contemptuous term for a woman.
4. **Chronicles.** 1,4. The history books; from Gk. meaning ' time '.
5. **Paucas pallabris.** 1,4–5. A blunder for Spanish ' pocus palabras ': few words.
6. **Sessa.** 1,5. Probably a cry used by way of exhorting to swift running—Schmidt.
7. **Denier.** 1,7. A French coin, the twelfth of a sou.
8. **Jeronimy.** 1,7. Sly's form of *Hieronimo*, the principal character in the ' Spanish Tragedy ' of Kyd.
9. **Third-borough.** 1,9. The petty-constable of a township or manor. He was formerly the head-man of a frank-pledge or system by means of which the whole tithing (a company of ten householders) was answerable for the good conduct of or damage done by any of its members.
10. **Emboss'd.** 1,13. Driven to extremity, exhausted, foaming at the mouth.
11. **Brach.** 1,14. A bitch-hound: pro-nounced ' braitch '. Formerly the name was applied only to a kind of hound that hunted by scent, but it is now generalized.
12. **Fault.** 1,16. ' Silver made it good . . . in the coldest fault '. A ' fault ' is a term in hunting meaning ' a break in the line of scent '. Hence the meaning is ' the worst of one of these breaks ', where the scent was very faint indeed.
13. **Merest.** 1,19. Complete. In the time of Shakespeare this word was used in its literal sense of **pure** (Lat. *merus* un-diluted, unmixed, pure), *real, actual.*
14. **Monstrous.** 1,32. ' O monstrous beast ! ' Abnormal, unnatural; from Lat. *monstrum* monster, which means 'something marvellous ' and formerly ' a divine warning or portent ', from the root of *monēre* to warn.
15. **Practise.** 1,34. Play a practical joke.
16. **Wanton.** 2,10. Amatory. The Lord is telling his servants to display his wanton pictures in Sly's bedchamber. The root meaning of the word is ' un-disciplined ' and is used in many varia-tions of this sense.
17. **Balm.** 2,11. Anoint. It is an archaic verb, meaning ' to embalm, anoint with fragrant, cleansing liquid, to soothe ', etc.
18. **Dulcet.** 2,14. Sweet; Fr.-Lat. *dulcis* sweet.
19. **Diaper.** 2,20. A piece of linen pat-terned with diamond shapes formed by the crossing directions of the thread. Ultimately from Gk. meaning *white*.
20. **Cunning.** 3,7. Capability; OE. *cunnan*, ME. *cunnen, connen* to know.
21. **Modesties.** 3,9. ' I am doubtful of your modesties '. Sense of delicacy and restraint.
22. **Over-eyeing.** 3,10. Examining.
23. **Merry passion.** 3,12. Expression of great amusement.
24. **Antic.** 3,16. ' Were he the veriest antic in the world '. Oddity. This word is from It. *antico* and was originally applied to the fantastic representation of human, animal and vegetable forms found in exhuming some ancient remains in Rome. It was not developed in England from ' antique ', but was a distinct use of the word from its first introduction.
25. **Buttery.** 3,17. The place where the food was kept; adapt. from OFr. *boterie = bouteillerie* from Lat. meaning ' a cask or bottle '. Hence ' a place for storing liquor ' and from an early period extended to ' the room where provisions are laid up '.
26. **Anon.** 3,45. Lit. ' at once ', but here meaning ' shortly '.
27. **Spleen.** 3,52. Sportiveness. The spleen was formerly thought to be the seat of the various impulses, melan-choly, laughter, impulse, courage, temper, etc.

GLOSSARY OF PHRASES

28. **I'll answer him by law.** 1,10. Give him a sound and lawful reason in reply to any charges he may make.
29. **How Silver made it good.** 1,15. Picked up the scent once again.
30. **He cried upon it at the merest loss.** 1,19. Picked it up after a complete loss. See note 13.
31. **Dress'd in all suits.** 3,21. Dressed in all particulars.

COMMENTARY

PART I SCENE II (Induction)

This scene is one of pure antithesis in the matter of treatment. SLY remains SLY in spite of silken coverlets, golden ewers, soft linen, elaborate ser-vants and every other form of luxury surrounding him. He is completely uninfluenced by anything except his thirst which calls for small ale, and his stomach which insists on beef instead of conserves ; and he insistently remains the possessor of only one doublet and the single articles of the rest of his outfit. Against this the LORD and SERVANTS display the most exaggerated forms of address and behaviour, in every particular carrying out the attempt to persuade SLY that he is indeed a lord, with the touch of the ludicrous which empha-sizes the situation. They all have to work very hard, but they have the figures of speech with which to carry out their task. Gradually they do convince SLY of his real dignity, and he proceeds in his conversion by a number of wondering questions, each spaced out to give his brain time to feel the fact to be true.

" *I do not sleep* . . ." This is realization awak-ing positively ; but it is taken by degrees as the facts slowly establish themselves in SLY's mind, each one receiving individual consideration, with a growing but subdued excitement making itself evident in the progress, until it issues unrestrained, in " *Upon my life, I am a lord indeed . . . Sly* ". However, lord or not, we have a sudden reversion to the tinker as he asks longingly for his " *pot of the smallest ale* ", just as himself.

Play the scene between SLY and the PAGE with-out any regard to the former's condition of lord-ship, whilst the PAGE must play up to him with regard to every required effect as the deeply obedient and longing wife, suddenly becoming very alert at SLY's somewhat indecorous inclina-tions. Thus the scene is carried through to the end in the same prevailing vein of natural absurdity but having reality for its basis.

GLOSSARY OF WORDS

32. **Small ale.** 4,1. Ale of a weak (cheap) quality.
33. **Sack.** 4,2. A general name for a class of dry white wines formerly imported from Spain and the Canaries.
34. **Conserves.** 4,4. Confections preserved in sugar, consisting of ginger or fruits.
35. **Doublets.** 4,9. The upper-body garments worn by men.
36. **Idle humour.** 4,12. Irresponsible condition of mind. In ancient and medieval physiology (a humour was) one of the four chief fluids . . . of the body (blood, phlegm, choler, and melancholy or black choler), by the relative proportions of which a person's physical and mental qualities and disposition were held to be determined— O.E.D. It was a word very much played with in Shakespeare's day.
37. **Card-maker.** 4,18. (Probably) a maker of playing-cards.
38. **Transmutation.** 4,18. ' By transmutation a bear-herd '. The word actually means ' a change of condition ' and is simply another way of saying that Sly became a bear-herd, one who leads a performing bear.
39. **Bear-herd.** 4,18. See preceding note.
40. **Sheer.** 4,21. ' Sheer ale '. Ale without food.
41. **Ancient thoughts.** 4,28. ' Call home thy ancient thoughts from banishment '. The Lord appeals to Sly to return to the wholesome condition of mind of happier days.
42. **Apollo.** 4,32. The son of Zeus and Leto. He was, amongst other things, the god of music.
43. **Semiramis.** 4,36. A famous queen in Assyria, wife of Ninus the founder of Nineveh. She was a great builder and warrior and made Babylon the most magnificent city of the world. Her charms were irresistible and she is reputed to have slain the young men who were called to her arms lest they bore witness to her licentiousness.

44. **Welkin.** 5,4. The vault of heaven; OE. *wolcen, wolcn* a cloud.
45. **Breathed.** 5,8. In good wind.
46. **Adonis.** 5,11. A beautiful young man, son of a king of Cyprus, born of his own daughter for refusing to pay tribute to Aphrodite. Aphrodite fell in love with him, and later when he was killed by a boar she caused the anemone to spring from his blood.
47. **Cytherea.** 5,12. Aphrodite was sometimes known as the Cytherean, from the name of the island Cythera on which she was supposed to have landed after her birth in the sea.
48. **Io.** 5,15. Daughter of Inachus, King of Argos. She was beloved by Zeus who turned her into a white heifer to hide her from his wife Hera. Hera sent Argus, the herdsman with a hundred eyes, to guard her, and when he was killed by Hermes, she sent a gadfly which goaded Io to long wanderings. She swam the Bosporus (Ox-ford) which was named after the event, and finally reached Egypt where she was restored to human shape and bore Zeus a son Epaphus who founded Memphis. In Egypt she was worshipped as Isis.
49. **Daphne.** 5,18. A nymph who was pursued by Apollo and was at her own entreaty changed into a laurel tree. The god crowned himself with the leaves of the tree and ordained that ever after it should be sacred to him.
50. **Waning.** 5,24. Degenerate, probably meaning that the one woman referred to is an exception to the declining beauty of women, and that Sly is very fortunate as things go.

51. **Fay. 5,43. Faith.** ' Faith ' was the original, but ' fey, fay ' also passed into English from contemporary Fr. (1300) and was for a time almost as common, especially in such phrases as *par fay, by my fay.*
52. **Rail. 5,48.** ' Rail upon the hostess of the house '. Cast abusive and violent language upon the hostess.
53. **Leet. 5,49.** ' And say you would present her at the leet '. A special kind of court of record which the lords of certain manors were empowered by charter or prescription to hold annually or semi-annually; = *court-leet.*
54. **Amends. 6,3.** ' My good amends '. Restoration to health.
55. **Goodman. 6,11.** Husband. It was formerly used as a title of dignity or respectful form of address to any man of quality.
56. **Congeal'd. 6,36.** ' Too much sadness hath congeal'd your blood '. Slowed it down, made him depressed and lacking vigour.
57. **Melancholy. 6,37.** One of the humours. See note 36.
58. **Frenzy. 6,37.** Madness.
59. **Comonty. 6,41.** Sly's version of ' comedy '.
60. **Gambold. 6,42.** Sly's alternative for *gambol,* lit. a frisky or leaping movement, and being a ' Christmas gambold ' it probably meant a festal dance.
61. **Household stuff. 6,44.** Something of a homely quality. The Page states that the comedy is more pleasing stuff than ' a Christmas gambold or a tumbling-trick '. Sly's reply is a slight quibble on the usual meaning of the phrase which is that of household furniture or goods and chattels. Only Sly knows why.
62. **History. 6,45.** A tale or drama.

GLOSSARY OF PHRASES

63. **Because she brought stone jugs and no seal'd quarts.** 5,50. Open jugs in which the measure of liquor could be incomplete as against those bearing an official seal guaranteeing that the proper quantity was intact.

COMMENTARY

PART I SCENE III

The Play

These first two scenes of the play proper, being introductory, do not contain major action. They must therefore be studied carefully so as to enable their material to develop its own interest, and the technical contrivances must be fully observed in order to effect this. Once the plot takes shape, it begins to wield the text with its own evident power. Here where we have talk alone concerned only in preparatory activity we must take particular care to regulate it so that it becomes stimulated into a lively form.

In this scene we have a pleasant succession of well defined episodes, each of a different nature. None is very deep, but side by side, they contribute to the general interest by their individual differences. Each has an engaging nature, and lasts just long enough so as not to exhaust itself. The opening episode presents the lively young LUCENTIO, happy and clean-spirited, telling us about himself in an easy, happy way, and growing a little steadier as he informs TRANIO that he has come to study virtue and philosophy. This gives a slight emphasis to the passage, sufficient to arouse a mild concern in TRANIO and a reason for asking his master not to be too strict in his methods and to allow for something of a good time as well. Keep the pace lively ; and, though colloquial and light, see that the matter is not starved of its details and lost in undistinguishable sameness. Though the surface is smooth, let us see a ripple and a slight play of action at work.

A complete contrast becomes the neighbour event with the genial but harassed BAPTISTA, the crabbed old GREMIO, the straightforward HORTENSIO, the hot-tempered, bitter KATHARINA, the obedient and gentle BIANCA all gathered together and operating in their contrasts one with the other. Here let it be pointed out that as far as the men are concerned, the characters of this play each possess a quaintness. None is perfectly straight. Natural, yes, most certainly and never otherwise, but they all exhibit a slight eccentricity in their composition. It is this which gives the charm and amusement to the play, and flavours each action with a uniqueness of quality. There is never any heaviness or depth to them but a certain delicacy of deviation from the normal without being farcical. The producer must devise these gentle abnormalities and balance them one with the other *because they do make the play*, and without them the situations drag.

The little romantic interjection made by LUCENTIO and TRANIO is very apt and just breaks up the incident sufficiently to vary the movement, and it must come in *at once* and must not linger.

BAPTISTA's address to HORTENSIO and GREMIO on the subject of cunning schoolmasters is definite but gentle, kindly and gratifying.

The scene between GREMIO and HORTENSIO must be played closely and with the points properly made without over-emphasis. Then again, and without any pause, we turn to LUCENTIO in love, and burning, pining, perishing with his passion. This points out the treatment required as opposed to the more practically minded TRANIO. LUCENTIO can only see sweet beauty in BIANCA's face and all that is sacred and sweet. He is lost in his trance and it is TRANIO who shows him that he has got to use something more than rapture if he wants to win the maid, and beats out the injunction to " Bend thoughts and *wits* to achieve her ". Thereon both become immediately active in this respect. This must be done with virility and pace. A solution is found, and with it an obstacle which momentarily exasperates them but is defeated with quick resourcefulness and a spirited unfolding of the plan. Pace, attack, the slight variations of treatment as cloud overshadows the ingenious workings of hope, excitement, and the speedy exchange of clothes as the plan matures into its first stage of accomplishment, all play their parts and make action alive.

In the scene with BIONDELLO care must be taken to avoid an anti-climax after the strenuous activity in the last incident. This is done, first by the introduction of a new character with an odd personality. He is derived from the traditional clown, but is not quite so freakish. He is a servant, alert, quick-witted, ingenious, possessing a lively sense of humour which here greets the change that he immediately sees has taken place between his fellow-servant and LUCENTIO. All this helps to take charge of the attention of the audience after the end of the last episode, and carry it forward in a sustained interest. Furthermore, LUCENTIO, now leaving his more excited efforts, trains his powers to the damping down of BIONDELLO's jesting mood, by emphasis in a slower, weightier form of treatment. By these means, substance is supplied that compensates the closing of one style of action with the introduction of another of equal grip and so allows the scene to continue without diminishing in power.

From this very brief survey it will be seen that there is a deliberate plan of composition serving in a determining capacity throughout the scene, varieties of character, of subject matter, of alternating methods of treatment which must be recognized and obeyed in order to allow the qualities of the scene to be presented to us in the fullness which makes it so attractive. Keep the episodes well knit together, *so that they follow closely on one another. Don't try to extract more than is in them by dwelling unduly upon them.* They are all very slight and that is why they are brief, but in their brevity make them complete in their features in the ways that have been suggested. Above all, keep the pace fairly fast except in those passages where the action is more deliberate.

GLOSSARY OF WORDS

64. **Ingenious studies.** 7,9. Studies in ingenious or highly intellectualized or artistic subjects.
65. **Great traffic.** 7,12. ' A merchant of great traffic through the world '. One with widespread commercial interests.
66. **Bentivolii.** 7,13. One of the great medieval Italian families.
67. **Plash.** 7,23. A shallow pool of water.
68. **Satiety.** 7,24. Full gratification. The more usual sense is that of over-indulgence, but each was used.
69. **Mi perdonato.** 7,25. Pardon me.
70. **Affected.** 7,26. ' I am in all affected as yourself '. Of the same mind as his master; adapt. from Lat. *affectāre* to aim at, aspire to, pretend to love.

71. **Stoics.** 7,31. A school of Gk. philosophers founded by Zeno, the doctrine of which was to bear pain, suffering and affliction with indifference.
72. **Stocks.** 7,31. Blocks of wood (without any warm, human and romantic feelings). The word primarily means ' a tree-trunk deprived of its branches ' or ' a tree-stump '.
73. **Aristotle.** 7,32. A famous Gk. philosopher, and pupil of Plato, afterwards founding his own schools. Among his writings is the celebrated treatise on Logic, probably referred to here.
74. **Ovid.** 7,33. A celebrated Roman poet famous for his amatory and romantic writings.

75. **Abjured.** 7,33. Renounced; lit. ' to deny on oath, swear away '.
76. **Stomach.** 7,38. Taste, inclination.
77. **Affect.** 7,40. See note 70.
78. **Gramercies.** 7,41. Lit. great thanks.
79. **Show.** 7,47. A spectacle, masque or pageant. It does not mean a play.
80. **Cart.** 8,6. ' To cart her rather '. Carry in a cart by way of punishment.
81. **Stale.** 8,9. ' To make a stale of me '. A fool. Lit. it means ' something used to entice ', primarily ' a pigeon to draw a hawk into the net '; hence ' something used to draw on or dupe, to use in an ignominious way '.
82. **Mates.** 8,9. A term of contempt.
83. **I wis.** 8,13. For certain. In reality the two words are one: **iwis.**

84. **Froward.** 8,20. Forward, self-assertive.

85. **Peat.** 8,29. ' A pretty peat ! ' Normally a term of endearment, but here used sarcastically. The origin is unknown.

86. **Discontent.** 8,31. ' Content you in my discontent '. Unhappiness, because Bianca cannot be married until Katharina has found a husband.

87. **Minerva.** 8,35. The Roman goddess of wisdom, war and the liberal arts. She sprang from Jupiter's brain after he had devoured his wife Metis lest her children should prove more exalted than their father.

88. **Strange.** 8,36. ' Signor Baptista, will you be so strange ? ' Perverse. Hortensio is questioning Baptista about his curious imposition respecting Bianca.

89. **Mew.** 8,39. Confine; orig. to put a hawk in a ' mew ', or cage, at moulting time.

90. **Cunning.** 8,49. See note 20.

91. **Commune.** 8,53. Discuss intimately with.

92. **Brooked parle.** 9,7. ' Though the nature of our quarrel yet never brooked parle '. Endured talking about; OE. *brucan* to enjoy, make use of.

93. **Lief.** 9,21. ' I had as lief take her dowry '. Soon; OE. *léof*, *liof* dear, beloved, hence ' something preferred in choice '.

94. **Dowry.** 9,21. The gift of money, property or goods that the wife brings as her marriage portion; Lat. *dōtāre* to endow.

95. **High cross.** 9,22. A cross set on steps in the market-place or centre of a town.

96. **Bar.** 9,24. ' This bar in law '. Legal obstruction. Hortensio and Gremio being both suitors to Bianca are confronted by the prohibitive ruling of the father against Bianca's marriage until Katharina has been married.

97. **Anna.** 9,40. Sister to Dido, queen of Carthage, and later deified.

98. **Chide.** 9,45. Reprove. This word fluctuated in meaning, and varied from that of loud and angry scolding to the gentler forms of reproof. Its primary meaning was that of the more forcible kind and it is used in this sense in the course of this play.

99. **Rated.** 9,46. ' Affection is not rated from the heart '. Controlled. The heart feels and what it feels has to be done. It acts from impulse, not reason.

100. **Longly.** 9,51. ' You looked so longly '. Longingly.

101. **Pith.** 9,52. ' The pith of all '. The reason for Baptista's strange ruling.

102. **Agenor.** 9,54. The father of Europa, whom Jupiter seduced by changing himself into a bull and mingling with her herds. She mounted its back in admiration of the animal and was carried across the sea to Crete.

103. **Shrewd.** 10,10. ' So curst and shrewd '. Bad-tempered, vicious. It was supposed that the shrew-mouse possessed malignant influences capable of affecting people with evil temper. The attribute of being vicious is probably derived from the supposed fact that it bit horses and caused them to die, or by passing over a beast's back caused it to become diseased in the spine.

104. **Advised.** 10,16. ' Art thou not advised '. Made aware; Fr.-Lat. source meaning ' view, opinion '. Lucentio is asking Tranio if he did not see or observe what Baptista did.

105. **Cunning.** 10,17. See note 20.

106. **Jump.** 10,21. Combine.

107. **Ply.** 10,29. ' Ply his book '. Keep up his studies. ' Ply ' is an aphetic form of ' apply ' and is here used as meaning ' to work at '.

108. **Basta.** 10,31. It. for ' enough '.

109. **Port.** 10,36. ' Keep house and port '. A good appearance and standard of living.

110. **Neapolitan.** 10,38. A man from Naples.

111. **Uncase.** 10,40. Undress.

112. **Sith.** 10,44. Seeing. It was very commonly used in this sense from c. 1500 to c. 1670, being frequently used to express cause, while ' since ' was restricted to time. It is a reduced form of OE. *siððan* ' subsequent to that '.

113. **Time.** 11,5. ' Frame your manners to the time '. Prevailing circumstances.

114. **Countenance.** 11,7. Condition, identity. The word orig. meant ' bearing, behaviour ', etc., adopt. from OFr.-Lat. *continentia* holding back, repression (of passions, desires, etc.), hence ' character '. The meaning became extended in Eng. to ' face, appearance as indicative of character ' but was still accompanied by the more literal sense as here.

115. **Descried.** 11,10. Seen and cried out upon.

116. **Whit.** 11,14. ' Ne'er a whit '. Not in the slightest particular.

117. **Discreetly.** 11,21. ' You use your manners discreetly '. Carefully, cautiously as circumstances demand. Tranio is instructing Biondello to behave himself with propriety.

GLOSSARY OF PHRASES

118. **I am arrived for fruitful Lombardy.** 7,3. He has exchanged or left the district of Lombardy for Padua which is in the province of Venice.

119. **All hopes conceived.** 7,15. The hopes entertained by his father.

120. **Balk logic with acquaintance.** 7,34. Bandy logic and find arguments in discourse with your friends. ' Balk ' is used in the sense of exercising logic in trivial arguments or conversations with his acquaintances. Note that the final ' s ' of the last word is omitted as is frequently the case in such terminations.

121. **Practise rhetoric in your common talk.** 7,35. Exercise rhetoric in ordinary conversation. Tranio is trying to persuade Lucentio to forego serious and isolated study and substitute the more commonplace kind in convivial company. He is tempting him to facile substitutes for the purpose of indulging in pleasure as well.

122. **I wis it is not half way to her heart.** 8,13. Katharina is merely telling Hortensio that her heart is in no way inclined towards him. The use of the third person singular instead of the first makes her more remote. See also note 83.

123. **Paint your face and use you like a fool.** 8,16. The combing of Hortensio's head with a stool would stain his face with blood and make it look like a fool's head or bauble.

124. **It is best Put finger in the eye, an she knew why.** 8,29-30. Cry like a baby, if she understood what it was all about. It is Katharina's caustic thrust at her sister so favoured by her father as against herself, and likening her to a little child in every particular.

125. **We may blow our nails together, and fast it fairly out.** 9,2. A proverbial expression meaning ' to be patient '.

126. **Our cake's dough on both sides.** 9,2-3. Their luck is quite out: another proverbial expression.

127. **There's small choice in rotten apples.** 9,23-4. A further proverbial way of saying that there seems to be small hope for them in their ambition.

128. **Happy man be his dole !** 9,27. A proverbial saying meaning a wish for good luck, or happiness will be to the one who succeeds. No precise literal version can be given but the second one suggested here suits the context.

129. **He that runs fastest gets the ring.** 9,28. The most resourceful one gets the prize.

130. **Love in idleness.** 9,37. The flower known as hearts-ease. Its juice was supposed to cause those on whose eyes it fell to fall in love at first sight.

131. **Redime te captum quam queas minimo.** 9,48. ' Buy thyself out of captivity for as little as thou canst ', an alteration of a line of Terence.

COMMENTARY

PART I SCENE IV

Throughout this scene we have a variety of incidents, each possessing a character of its own, and each basically requiring a virile treatment. As in the previous scenes, although each episode has a specific interest, none is so complex or weighty as to demand any measured consideration. If this is done the effect will be that of slowness and inefficiency because the matter is not severe enough to warrant prolonged or serious deliberation. The virtue here lies in pace, close-playing, entertainment and not instruction.

In the opening chapter we have our first meeting with PETRUCHIO. He too is a young man, a spirited young man, but also a very charming one. Also, he possesses a rich sense of humour. *Both these qualities are very valuable to his character and the entire action of the play.* He knows his mind and can assert it, but it is always with these two special qualities, charm and humour, abiding in it. This is a very important thing to remember because upon this fact the whole *nature* of the ensuing plot depends. PETRUCHIO is not a bully. He tames KATHARINA by his personality as emphasized by the foregoing characteristics. A woman of KATHARINA's temperament would not yield to violence, neither would the play be acceptable if this were the theme. PETRUCHIO is no woman-beater and we do not want any suggestion that he is so. He establishes himself in his first scene as a happy, high-spirited youthful adventurer in life, ready to tease his servant, if a little roughly, yet in a good-humoured way, greeting his friend with a warm heart and unfolding his intentions in a few concise sentences, but all happily and tightly told. Swiftness, sureness, colloquiality and perfect ease of manner are the main characteristics of this early action in the scene. It is the nature of the man and of the play. It *is* the action. But do not merely rush through in order to cover the ground. Make everything *intelligent.* Let the words be heard clearly and meaningly even though they are swift. HORTENSIO must keep pace with PETRUCHIO and not drag in treatment. His speech "*Petruchio, shall I then come roundly to thee*" is made as a jest in answer to PETRUCHIO's intimation that he is looking for a wife. He knows of a wife all right, shrewish but rich. The jest however may be a feeler for his purpose as well. This element is indicated by his opening two lines which are less swift and more deliberate. This also applies to his lines, "*And yet I'll promise . . . and very rich*", emphasizing an attractive proposition, if money is the persuading element. This helps to steady the action somewhat, which at the same time stimulates itself by its introduction of possibilities made in a jesting way. GRUMIO also assists in this steadying process, because his own manner and matter are individual and are quite sufficient to hold the attention. Also he gives a variety to the prevailing temperament of the scene between the other two.

HORTENSIO gets deftly busy at "*Petruchio . . . thus far in*". This is the real maturing of plot. He does not draw his speech out so much as particularizes the details. "*I can, Petruchio . . . wife*" is made a very definite fact. He paints KATHARINA's qualities without reserve, but the undaunted PETRUCHIO comes right in with relish, for here is an adventure after his own heart. HORTENSIO, seeing this, strenuously supplies further details. PETRUCHIO finds that he already has a ready-made opening to further acquaintance with the family concerned and is at the height of

resolve to start operations *instantly.* All this variety of action gives us a slightly broken surface in a passage of necessarily swift tempo of speech, and enables an appreciable action to assert itself in very mild dramatic form.

Something of a minor climax having been reached, the action has to take a new direction. The change must not be too abrupt, and so GRUMIO with his less agile but still forceful temperament comes in with a buffer speech, out of which the steadier movement as contained in HORTENSIO's speech then emerges. This technical evolution enables the scene to calm down to a more practical nature and at the same time anticipate a complete change shortly to come. HORTENSIO has to set forth some very essential details which he does with precision and by using a moderate pace in order to achieve his purpose. He keeps his delivery lively and pointed, but not too hurried. We are now listening to plot.

Then comes the change in the nature of the scene already alluded to which would be too abrupt unless approached in the manner shown. This guarded process is a prevalent characteristic of Shakespeare's work in comedy and tragedy alike. The strenuous element has lasted long enough, and a new one takes its place. What we require is something more leisurely, but interesting. Leisure is welcome, but it must also be attractive. GREMIO, old, somewhat excited, and very anxious to insure that LUCENTIO knows exactly what he has to do, works hard at his task, and LUCENTIO is assurance itself in compliance with his duties. Then GREMIO and HORTENSIO meet and exchange their achievements, which little pleasant talk suddenly wakens into a flash of rivalry. Then PETRUCHIO is again brought into the scene and the plot joins its component parts and begins to warm up. Characters and situations hitherto exploited singly and kept apart, are now combined, and the action, rested from its early swiftness, is vigorously resumed as the various individualities respond to each other. Hence the values of the treatment that has been appropriated to the introductory developments which, though only lightly sketched in, should lead the thoughtful reader to realize something of the importance of mechanics in art and what contributes to the successful fulfilling of the just effect. He will also realize the pertinence of the remarks made in the Foreword.

PETRUCHIO issues from the new event in a speech whose figures are designed to make it happily brave and resounding, as the situation demands. Take it without too much vociferousness, and rather work at the descriptive features to give a sense of the threatening significance of each, than either rattle off the text as a piece of sounding brass or feature it with theatrical isolation. Base it first as a piece of conversation and add the worth of the words in exploitation of the singular nature of each item. This will not only be better for the general effect but will also enable PETRUCHIO to retain his appeal, which over-stylization would obscure.

A short buffer interlude then occurs to lower the pitch of PETRUCHIO's speech and lead the action into other hands. It is taken with great gratification, which gives it life and brings us to the entrance of TRANIO impersonating LUCENTIO. The substance of this scene in its beginning is the manner of TRANIO's behaviour. Here, again, the artist is required. It is slightly, but *only slightly*, overdrawn as a study of lofty self-assurance and self-assertiveness in contact with the other interested

parties. He takes the stage completely as a man of means and position and with ability to hold his own and boldly assert his right to woo BIANCA as well as anyone else. This quality amuses us *if properly* simulated and also offers the other characters the means to register their own values in opposition to his. HORTENSIO and GREMIO have in consequence of this a short passage of arms which could not breed except out of the irritation caused by TRANIO's manner of expressing himself.

Contact with PETRUCHIO brings him into a warm and spirited gratitude for the opportunity which the latter offers to enable BIANCA to be wooed, and the whole company ends the scene with great and happy anticipation of intense but friendly rivalry to be begun with a merry afternoon of quaffing carouses to their mistress' healths.

GLOSSARY OF WORDS

132. **Trow.** 11,30. Believe; OE. *tréowan, tréowian* from *tréowe* faith, belief.
133. **Rebused.** 11,33. Grumio's blunder for ' abused '.
134. **Ring.** 12,5. ' I'll ring it '. He will ring Grumio's ear and so announce his presence by the ' bell ' of Grumio's cries.
135. **Sol, fa.** 12,6. Using the nouns of notation as verbs.
136. **Compound.** 12,16. Compose, heal; from Lat. meaning ' to place or put together '.
137. **'Leges.** 12,17. ' What he 'leges in Latin '. Alleges or declares. Grumio, being thoroughly English, takes Italian to be Latin.
138. **Pip.** 12,21. ' A pip out '. A pip of a boy.
139. **Maze.** 12,41. Maze or puzzle-path of a world where the way to fortune needs finding out after many mistakes.
140. **Haply.** 12,42. By (good) fortune; ME. adopt. from O.Norse *happ* chance, good luck.
141. **Crowns.** 12,43. A crown was equal to five shillings.
142. **Shrewd.** 12,46. See note 103.
143. **Florentius.** 13,1. The name of a knight in Gower's *Confessio Amantis.* ' Florentius bound himself to marry a deformed hag, provided she taught him the solution of a riddle on which his life depended '—Nares.
144. **Sibyl.** 13,2. The most ancient and celebrated of the ten Sibyls, who were prophetesses inspired by a deity— usually Apollo—was Herophile of Erythraea, also identified with Cumaea. Apollo desired her and offered her a gift. She chose a life equal in years to the number of grains of sand she held in her hand. Unfortunately she forgot to ask for continuing youth and health at the same time. She was reputed to have lived a thousand years.
145. **Xanthippe.** 13,3. The wife of Socrates, the famous Greek philosopher, and celebrated for her scolding tongue. The name is pronounced ' Xantippe '.
146. **Puppet.** 13,10. A contemptuous term for a woman without sense or quality.
147. **Aglet-baby.** 13,10-11. A grown-up baby-type of woman decked with aglets, which are the metal tags at the end of laces. The exact meaning is not established. It may mean ' overdressed ', or one affecting the styles of youth when past the appropriate age— ' fancy goods '.
148. **Trot.** 13,11. Hag. The derivation is uncertain.

149. **Shrewd.** 13,21. See note 103.
150. **Froward.** 13,21. See note 84.
151. **Chide.** 13,26. See note 98. The meaning here is the more forceful one.
152. **Humour.** 13,38. See note 36.
153. **Rail.** 13,41. See note 52.
154. **Other more.** 13,50. Others as well.
155. **Proper.** 14,15. ' A proper stripling '. Handsome young man.
156. **Amorous.** 14,15. Engaging, attractive.
157. **Largess.** 14,22. Bounty; adopt. from Fr. *largesse*—Late Lat. *largitia* from *largus* abundant, bountiful, profuse.
158. **Patron.** 14,27. ' I'll plead for you As for my patron '. ' The one in whose interests I am working '. It is eventually derived from Lat. *patrōn-us* protector, defender, a derivative of *pater, patr-em* father. Its more usual application is in the sense of someone of distinction who favours and supports another with his influence in some enterprise. The present meaning seems to be adapted from the ancient Roman practice of giving protection and aid to a client in return for certain services.
159. **Still.** 14,28. Always, a prevalent adverbial meaning in Shakespeare.
160. **Woodcock.** 14,32. ' O this woodcock, what an ass it is ! ' Grumio likens Lucentio to a woodcock because of the ease with which that bird is trapped. He knows what is going on and that Hortensio is also doing the same thing and for the same purpose.
161. **Trow.** 14,36. See note 132.
162. **Bags.** 14,49. Money bags.
163. **Vent.** 14,50. ' 'Tis now no time to vent our love '. Exercise in terms of rivalry. ' Vent ' means ' to express, pour forth ', etc., but the context contains the sense of doing so in opposition to one another.
164. **Indifferent.** 14,52. ' I'll tell you news indifferent good for either '. Equally good, without difference or advantage for either.
165. **Dowry.** 15,2. See note 94.
166. **Stomach.** 15,12. See note 76.
167. **Chafed.** 15,21. ' Chafed with sweat '. Hot. The root meaning of ' chafe ' is ' to heat, make warm '.
168. **Ordnance.** 15,22. Artillery. It is used to avoid duplication with the synonym in the following line.
169. **Bugs.** 15,29. ' Fear boys with bugs '. Bugbears, scarecrows. Bugbear by itself probably means ' ghost '.

170. **Chides.** 15,45. See note 98. The meaning here is probably the forceful one.
171. **Leda.** 16,11. Wife of Tyndarus, King of Sparta. She was wooed by Zeus in the guise of a swan. One of her children was Helen, later abducted by Paris of Troy.
172. **Paris.** 16,14. Son of Priam, King of Troy. He was an extremely handsome young man and abducted Helen.
173. **Speed.** 16,14. ' Though Paris came in hope to speed alone '. Profit, win the lady; from OE. *spówan* to prosper, succeed.
174. **Jade.** 16,16. Any inferior kind of horse, one given to his own whims.
175. **Hercules.** 16,24. The Roman equivalent of Heracles, the celebrated Greek hero ; son of Zeus and Alcmena (the wife of Amphitryon). To expiate the crime of destroying his wife and children in a fit of madness he was ordered by an Oracle to submit to Eurytheus, King of Argos, who set him to perform twelve great labours.
176. **Alcides.** 16,25. A name applied to the descendants of Alcaeus. In this case Hercules. His stepfather was Amphitryon the son of Alcaeus, who was himself a son of Perseus.
177. **Stead.** 16,33. ' You are the man Must stead us all '. Help; lit. place us (in our objective). The verb is formed from the OE. verb *stede* place.
178. **Achieve.** 16,35. ' Achieve the elder '. Secure the elder daughter as a wife.
179. **Access.** 16,36. ' Set the younger free For our access '. Liberty of approach, the ban on this being removed by the fact that Katharina will have been married.
180. **Hap.** 16,36. See note 140.
181. **Ingrate.** 16,37. Unthankful; adapt. from Lat. *ingrāt-us* unpleasing, ungrateful.
182. **Gratify.** 16,40. Show gratitude and appreciation.
183. **Quaff carouses.** 16,44. Drink deeply and in a thorough way. ' To quaff ' means ' to drink copiously, in a long draught '; and a ' carouse ' is ' a drinking bout wherein the participants go all out '. The origin of the first is obscure; the second is of German origin.
184. **Motion.** 16,47. Proposal, suggestion, something moved as an idea. Grumio welcomes the idea made by Tranio that all parties should quaff carouses and eat and drink generously.
185. **Ben venuto.** 16,50. Welcome.

GLOSSARY OF PHRASES

186. **Knock you here, sir !** 11,35. Grumio is deliberately punning upon Petruchio's line ' Here, sirrah Grumio; knock, I say ', meaning that he should knock at the door of the house. He now contorts it into implying that he has been asked to knock his master down in the public street.

187. **I should knock you first.** 12,1–2. ' I should do as you ask and then get something far worse from you '. He can see through his master's little manœuvre. An accent is required on ' after ' in order to develop the sense of this.

188. **Con tutto il cuore, ben trovato.** 12,13. ' With all my heart, well met '.

189. **Alla nostra casa ben venuto, molto honorato signor mio Petruchio.** 12,14–15. ' Welcome to our house, my much honoured Petruchio '.

190. **He'll rail in his rope-tricks.** 13,41–2. Bawl out in violent

or abusive language when dealing with Katharina as he would with a horse when being broken in to the halter. Also there is a pun on ' rope-tricks ' which suggests ' rhetorics ' or forceful speech.

191. **An she stand him but a little . . . than a cat.** 13,42–4. If she stands up to him in the slightest way he will use some figure of speech that will liken her figure to some animal so forcibly that she will only see herself as a cat. This is a play upon the contemporary similarity of pronunciation of ' Kate ' and ' cat ', the ' a ' being broad and long. Grumio foretells what is to come.

192. **And that his bags shall prove.** 14,49. It will prove to be Gremio's money-bags that will speak more eloquently than the deeds which he professes he will use to win Bianca's love.

193. **Give him head.** 16,16. Let him have his own way.

COMMENTARY

PART I SCENE V

The opening episodes between KATHARINA and BIANCO and BAPTISTA are straightforward enough not to need any detailed attention. They consist of contrasts. Bearing in mind the fact that the nature of the play asks for a slight out-of-the-ordinary style of characterization, especially as far as the men are concerned (this has already been pointed out in an earlier note), avoid making BAPTISTA a ' straight ' type of father. He is a very kindly old gentleman who can be sharp on occasion, but is never far away from affability and would be a contented old soul if this problem of a shrewish daughter could only be solved. Although not senile, he is on the elderly side, being the accepted traditional type as regards age, which was always quite definitely somewhat older than present conceptions would call for. He is a gentleman and courteous, mentally alert and quite able to manage his own affairs. By this means he has a distinctive quality of his own which allows him greater scope of style and effect in his concerns with the other characters. For instance, his soft but hearty greeting of his guests as they enter the chamber gives a greater effect of PETRUCHIO's immediate and blunt enquiry about his having a daughter " Call'd Katharina, fair and virtuous ", to which he replies with embarrassed hesitancy. It is not possible to dwell upon the details of this particular treatment throughout the scene, but it should be borne in mind and applied when studying the past.

Having examined the other characters previously, their characteristics must now be taken for granted. PETRUCHIO is, as we have seen him before, quick, clean and direct, wasting no time, but always maintaining his pleasant charm and easiness. TRANIO is, again, very much on his dignity and carries himself with conviction. In PETRUCHIO's speech " why, that is nothing " develop a little extra touch of virility and dauntlessness. This will add to the challenge of the response when

HORTENSIO appears " with his head broken ", and tells his tale of woe with graphic feeling. PETRUCHIO's admiration for KATHARINA's spirit is full and joyous and he is brimming over with eagerness to encounter her.

In his speech previous to her entrance, he rehearses all that he is going to do with delight. There is no sternness, but a sense of humour very pleasantly, but very precisely, presiding over the sure ordering of events. His salutation to her is short, sweet and abruptly familiar, but not forced. His speech, " You lie, in faith ", is all taken very pleasantly, the opening correction being effective through its sheer simplicity because this is so new to KATHARINA and is quite enough in itself. She is told the other facts contained in these two lines in the same simple but slightly whimsical way. After that PETRUCHIO proceeds lightly and pleasantly and almost daintily.

The passage on the whole of page 21 is just a conflict between the two characters, carried through with pace and vigour, PETRUCHIO controlling the situation with unoffended humour at KATHARINA's bitter anger. Even his reprimands are without severity, and are just politely cautionary. This good-natured toleration goes right through this actual ' wooing ' scene and it would not be possible to play it otherwise and gain the same artistic entertainment from it. The strong man is stronger where strength can be gently used and we don't get anywhere if two people are using violence. In the speech, " Marry, so I mean, sweet Katharina . . .", when he reaches " Thus in plain terms ", he does take a stronger grip upon her, good-natured but now obviously determined. This enables the speech to end the episode on a firm and conclusive note.

Throughout the following incident, PETRUCHIO continues his method of treating the situation with great humour, but now with the assumption that KATHARINA's shrewishness is all pretence. This he announces as though it were a real and vital discovery, and so we have the intenser form of subtle ridicule building up the interest, and handled with relish. This continues throughout the remainder of the episode, a slighter measure of emphasis being placed on " *'Tis bargain'd 'twixt us twain. . . .*" After that, the fictions are given imaginative over-drawing ; and then to conclude, comes the sudden and determined seizure of KATHARINA'S hand as an affianced woman, and the orders to prepare for the wedding, and the announcement of the *immediate* wedding-day. All this is done with great spirit and glee and final authority, and the episode ends with everyone as happy as they can be.

In the following ' bargaining ' scene, the main point to observe is to make the distinctions between GREMIO and TRANIO as clear as possible. As they are diverse in character, the old crabbedly old, the other boldly young, so their treatment varies. Both are angling for a very attractive prize. GREMIO tells his catalogue of possessions with great care of detail and appreciative treatment of each one, taking his time to make their worthiness known to BAPTISTA, whilst TRANIO swells with his boastfulness in easy stride. We then have conflict in character made as marked as possible.

GLOSSARY OF WORDS

194. **Gawds.** 17,3. Trinkets, jewellery or any form of trifling, showy ornamentation; probably adapt. from A.Fr.–Lat. *gaudére* to rejoice.
195. **Dissemble.** 17,9. Deceive. Lit. ' false show '.
196. **Minion.** 17,13. Lit. ' someone˜beloved, a darling ', but also used, as here, as a term of contempt: a jade, a ' creature ', flattering for favour.
197. **Affect.** 17,14. Desire. See also note 70.
198. **Ply.** 17,25. See note 107.
199. **Hilding.** 17,26. A contemptible creature; etymology obscure.
200. **Flouts.** 17,29. Mocks.
201. **Suffer.** 17,31. Be kindly disposed towards..
202. **Bare-foot.** 17,33. Like a humble country girl.
203. **Orderly.** 18,6. ' Go to it orderly '. Taking things by degrees, step by step.
204. **Cunning.** 18,17. See note 20.
205. **Turn.** 18,24. Suitability.
206. **Petitioners.** 18,33. Those seeking favours.
207. **Beccare.** 18,34. This is a misprint and should be ' Baccare ', an exclamation signifying ' go back ' and supposed to be a corruption of ' back there '. It was not confined to Shakespeare—Halliwell's Dictionary of Archaic and Provincial Words.
208. **Fain.** 18,35. Gladly; OE. *faeʒen*, *faeʒn* to rejoice.
209. **Methinks.** 18,45. It seems to me; from OE. *me* and 3rd person singular of *pyncan* (*thincan*) to seem. ' To think ' comes from OE. *pencan* (*thencan*).
210. **Stranger.** 18,46. One detached and alone.
211. **Preferment.** 18,52. Giving the first consideration to.
212. **Passing.** 19,16. ' You are passing welcome '. Very, extremely. The meaning is now obsolete.
213. **Dowry.** 19,24. See note 94.
214. **Crowns.** 19,26. See note 141.
215. **Leases.** 19,29. Lands leased to others for rent; hence ' rents '.
216. **Specialities.** 19,30. Lists of details in contract form.
217. **Covenants.** 19,31. Signed and sealed assurances.
218. **Peremptory.** 19,35. Completely determined. The word is adapt. from Lat. *peremptori -us* destructive, deadly, that puts an end to; *hence* unquestionably final. The accent is on the first syllable.
219. **Speed.** 19,42. See note 173.
220. **Frets.** 20,6. The metal or wooden narrow strips that run across the neck of a guitar and similar instrument and that act as stops whereby the fingering is regulated.

221. **Bow'd.** 20,7. Shaped it as required for the purpose.
222. **Fume.** 20,9. ' I'll fume with them '. This is an application of the phrase ' fret and fume ', meaning ' to give way to anger '. ' Fret ' in this phrase is from the verb meaning ' to irritate ', lit. ' eat away '. It is of course a play upon the word in its double meaning.
223. **Twangling Jack.** 20,15. Itinerant player, one whose skill does not rise beyond that of a rudimentary player. ' Jack ' was the name applied to a member of the common class.
224. **Lusty.** 20,17. Vigorously spirited.
225. **Volubility.** 20,33. Readiness and dexterity of speech. It is eventually from Lat. meaning ' to turn (with aptitude) '.
226. **Dainties.** 20,47. ' For dainties are all Kates '. A play upon ' Kate ' and ' cates ', the latter being particularly delicate and choice foods.
227. **Join'd-stool.** 21,2. Joint-stool; one joined together by a craftsman as opposed to the work of less refined quality. Katharina may be retorting that he is made of wood and about as sensible and worthy.
228. **Jade.** 21,6. See note 174. Here the meaning is ' a worthless person '.
229. **Burden.** 21,7. ' I will not burden thee '. A coarse quibble.
230. **Light.** 21,8. Slender, with a double meaning of ' light in moral restraint '.
231. **Swain.** 21,9. ' Too light for such a swain as you to catch '. A pun on ' light ' (light of foot) and inferring that Petruchio is a heavy-footed, clumsy rustic.
232. **Buzzard.** 21,12. Worthless, ignorant individual. A ' buzzard ' is an inferior kind of hawk useless for falconry. See also notes 296, 297.
233. **Turtle.** 21,13. ' O slow-wing'd turtle '. A turtle-dove, the emblem of conjugal affection and constancy, slow in flight. See also notes 296, 297.
234. **Herald.** 21,32. ' A herald, Kate ? ' Petruchio is referring to her statement about a gentleman and his (coat of) arms—see notes 300, 301. This is an heraldic point.
235. **Crest.** 21,33. ' What is your crest ? ' Strictly speaking the personal emblem of anyone of noble family, as distinct from his coat of arms or badge. It surmounted his helmet.
236. **Coxcomb.** 21,33. The comb of a cockerel, the ' crest ' of a fool, which surmounted his cap.
237. **Combless.** 21,34. ' A combless cock '. He will adopt a cock without a comb as his crest, showing that he has (willingly) lowered his pride in her favour.
238. **Craven.** 21,35. One who is beaten.

239. **Crab.** 21,37. Crab-apple, which is bitter to the taste. It is Katharina's retort to Petruchio who says that she looks sour.
240. **Wither'd.** 21,45. Bitter in tongue. This is Katharina's retort to Petruchio's inference that she is much too old for his attentions.
241. **Chafe.** 21,49. See note 167. Here the meaning is ' hot with temper '.
242. **Whit.** 21,50. See note 116.
243. **Coy.** 21,51. Repellent towards any masculine attentions.
244. **Sullen.** 21,51. Given to dark moods. It is a later form of *solein* adopt. from OFr. *solein*, *solain*, a derivative of *sol* sole. Hence ' singular, strange, unusual, aloof '.
245. **Halt.** 22,7. ' Thou dost not halt.' A pun on the double meaning of ' halt ': (*a*) to stop; (*b*) to limp. Katharina has been and should be continuing to walk about the room in a spirited way, like a young horse, or at least that is how Petruchio figures her. He is admiring her as such and comments upon her faultless condition.
246. **Dian.** 22,9. Diana was the Roman goddess of hunting and the moon. She was identified with the Greek Artemis, and was sister to Apollo. Her chastity is derived from her horror at the pain she caused her mother at her birth.
247. **Extempore.** 22,14. Lit. out of the present moment, straight out of the mind without any preparation.
248. **Nill.** 22,22. ' Will you, nill you '. ' Be you willing, be you unwilling '. The verb ' to nill ' means ' not to will ', from OE. *nylle*.
249. **Wild Kate.** 22,28. See note 191. We now have a pun on the person and the animal.
250. **Swearing Jack.** 22,40. One who swears or uses the uncouth language of a low type of individual.
251. **Policy.** 22,44. A set purpose.
252. **Froward.** 22,45. See note 84.
253. **Hot.** 22,46. Hot-tempered.
254. **Grissel.** 22,47. The name of the heroine of a tale of Chaucer's (the Clerk of Oxenford's Tale), proverbially known as the pattern of patience.
255. **Lucrece.** 22,48. Lucretia, the daughter of Lucretius, the celebrated Roman poet and philosopher. She was the wife of Tarquinius Collatinus and showed herself to be the pattern of constant virtue among the loose prevailing morals of ·other women of the time. She was ravished by Sextus, son of Tarquinius Superbus, and in the morning she declared to her husband and father what had happened, and stabbed herself to death.
256. **Speeding.** 22,53. See note 173. The

word is here played upon in its sense of 'profit' and the extended sense of 'haste'.

257. **Vied.** 23,6. 'She vied so fast'. Competed, tried to out-do in affection. It comes from Fr., meaning 'to increase the stake in card-playing, challenge, venture, bid'. Katharina, according to Petruchio, was most vehement in her amiable response to his affection.

258. **Twink.** 23,7. A second, the time taken by a winking of the eye.

259. **Novices.** 23,8. 'O, you are novices!' Inapt, inexperienced (in affairs of love and the management of women). Petruchio applauds his own resourcefulness in dealing with Kate, as against the inaptitude of the others.

260. **Meacock.** 23,10. 'A meacock wretch'. Effeminate, cowardly. The origin is obscure.

261. **Skipper.** 23,37. One who 'skips' with irresponsibility.

262. **Compound.** 23,39. See note 136.

263. **Ewers.** 23,46. Jugs with wide lips, containing water.

264. **Lave.** 23,46. Wash.

265. **Tyrian tapestry.** 23,47. Probably tapestry woven by Oriental weavers of which there was a large number in Venice at this time, and their work was extremely beautiful.

266. **Crowns.** 23,48. See note 141.

267. **Cypress chests.** 23,49. Chests made

of cypress wood which was frequently used for the purpose, and was of fine quality.

268. **Arras.** 23,49. Chiefly wall-hangings named after Arras in northern France, renowned for the richness of its tapestry fabrics.

269. **Counterpoints.** 23,49. Counterpanes. This word became altered to the later form about 1600, both being used concurrently until the end of the century when the first form disappeared. Lit. it means 'quilt stabbed or stitched through, quilted mattress'.

270. **Turkey cushions.** 23,51. Large, luxurious cushions of rich design made in Turkey.

271. **Boss'd.** 23,51. Ornamented.

272. **Valance.** 23,52. The border of drapery hanging round the top of a bed. The origin of the word is obscure.

273. **Milch-kine.** 24,1. Milking-cows; *milch* lit. means 'milk-giving'. 'Kine' is the archaic plural of 'cow'.

274. **Ducats.** 24,13. Gold coins of varying value formerly in use in most European countries. The Italian ducat was valued at about 3s. 6d. The word ultimately comes from Lat. *dux* duke.

275. **Jointure.** 24,14. His estate which she will share with him.

276. **Argosy.** 24,18. Large merchant ship, especially those of Ragusa and Venice; apparently adapt. from It. *Ragusa*. The transposition into 'argosea' is no doubt connected with the fact that in

16 thc. English, 'Ragusa' appears as 'Aragouse, Arrogonese, Arragossa'.

277. **Road.** 24,19. 'Marseilles' road'. The sheltered waters near the shore of the city where ships can anchor in safety.

278. **Choked.** 24,20. 'Have I choked you with an argosy?' A pun: (a) because of the excessive size of the ship; (b) because of the riches it represents.

279. **Galliases.** 24,22. Adapt. through Fr. from It. *galeazza*, augmentative of *gallea* 'galley'. A heavy, low-built vessel, larger than a galley, impelled both by sail and oars, chiefly employed in war.

280. **Tight.** 24,23. Trim and sound.

281. **Galleys.** 24,23. A smaller type of gallias. See note 279.

282. **Out-vied.** 24,29. See note 257.

283. **Assurance.** 24,31. Solemn pledge either in writing or before witnesses.

284. **Cavil.** 24,34. Frivolous, unreasonable; adopt. from OFr. meaning 'to mock, jest', etc.

285. **Gamester.** 24,45. Gambler.

286. **Waning.** 24,26. Declining. See note 50.

287. **Toy.** 24,47. 'Tut, a toy!' A piece of nonsense. Gremio tells Tranio that his father is not such a fool as to have given him all that he says he has to give to Bianca.

288. **Card of ten.** 24,50. A card that has ten pips; hence, according to its function in some game, the phrase is used to signify 'to brag, put on a bold front'.

GLOSSARY OF PHRASES

289. **Lead apes in hell.** 17,34. A proverbial expression meaning to die an old maid or a bachelor, this occupation jocularly being supposed to be appointed to such hereafter—Halliwell.

290. **Iron may hold with her.** 20,3. The handling of weapons may be more to her liking.

291. **Thou canst not break her to the lute.** 20,4. Bring her to submit to a study of it.

292. **For she hath broke the lute to me.** 20,5. Tranio adapts the word 'break' to a more practical meaning.

293. **Kate of my consolation.** 20,48. (Perhaps) the chief contribution to Petruchio's happiness. 'Kate' here may still be associated with 'cate'. See note 226.

294. **And yet as heavy as my weight should be.** 21,10. Balanced and steadied (weighted) with moral stability, not given to 'light' desires.

295. **Should be! should—buzz!** 21,11. Petruchio quibbles on the world 'should' as though she should be so but is not. 'Buzz' is said in the Variorum Shakespeare (1803) to have been a common exclamation (of impatience or contempt) when one was telling an unknown story. Schmidt and others say 'a sound to command silence'—OED. Here Petruchio is playfully taunting Katharina with his equivocation and expresses himself in this manner.

296. **O slow-wing'd turtle! shall a buzzard take thee?** 21,13. Petruchio retorts to Katharina's jibe that he is a buzzard, after his buzzing, by asking if such a mean bird as a buzzard should capture such a beautiful creature—implying that he is something better than a buzzard.

297. **Ay, for a turtle, as he takes a buzzard.** 21,14. Yes, for something inferior, as the turtle takes or regards the buzzard. Katharina is contemptuous of the thought of being a turtledove, such as Petruchio takes her to be, and qualifies his own inferiority as the (unconsciously) self-styled, although not consciously self-implied, buzzard.

298. **If you talk of tails.** 21,23. Because his sting is in his tongue.

299. **With my tongue in your tail.** 21,24. An obscene quibble. See suggested omissions at the end of this scene glossary.

300. **So may you lose your arms.** 21,28. A quibble on arms as limbs and as a coat of arms.

301. **And if no gentleman, why then no arms?** 21,31. If he strikes her he is no gentleman, and as such he cannot bear heraldic arms, because none below that rank could possess them. It was the office of the heralds to decide upon the granting of arms.

302. **Put me in thy books.** 21,32. 'Put me in your good favour as a herald to an applicant for arms'.

303. **Well aim'd of such a young one.** 21,43. A very intelligent answer for such a youngster.

304. **I am too young for you.** 21,44. Petruchio hits back by suggesting (a) that she is much older than he his, (b) that he is more agile in wit than she is.

305. **And then let Kate be chaste and Dian sportful.** 22,12. Then Kate can remain chaste and unmarried and Diana can become otherwise. See note 246.

306. **Witless else her son.** 22,15. Petruchio says that his retorts come out of his mother-wit. Katharina says that the mother is witty but not the son.

307. **Keep you warm.** 22,17. (Perhaps) keep yourself warm, or, being so slight, your wisdom will perish.

308. **Venture madly on a desperate mart.** 23,24. He gambles precipitately with a chance of disposing of an almost unmarketable commodity. 'Mart' is the same as 'market' and is used here to denote the commodity being marketed, and its unmarketable qualities.

309. **'Twas a commodity lay fretting by you.** 23,25. It was a piece of merchandise that lay 'eating its head off'.

310. **No doubt but he hath got a quiet catch.** 23,28. Gremio remarks that Petruchio seems to have been able to subdue Katharina.

311. **Greybeard, thy love doth freeze.** 23,35. Tranio informs Gremio that his love lacks passion, to which Gremio retorts that his rival's love is so hot that it shrivels to ineffectualness.

312. **And all things answerable to this portion.** 24,3. All things that go to make up the home with which Bianca will inherit.

313. **Set foot under thy table.** 24,47. Live as a dependant.

314. **An old Italian fox is not so kind.** 24,48. As Tranio's supposed father was obviously a clever man of business, he would not be so likely to give up everything to an inexperienced young man with impulse in his veins.

SUGGESTED OMISSIONS

P. 21. The following cuts in the text on this page are suggested:—
(1) From and including the sixth line, 'No such jade as you . .' up to and including the fourteenth line ending 'as he takes a buzzard'.

(2) From and including the sixteenth line, 'If I be waspish . . .' up to and including the twenty-fifth line ending '. . . nay, come again'.

COMMENTARY

PART I SCENE VI

This scene is quite straightforward and plainly declares itself. Like the previous scenes, it must be played with fullness and not modernized into pettiness. HORTENSIO and LUCENTIO open it with cutting rivalry, in which the language is used to the full advantage. BIANCA intervenes and calms the storm.

The main action lies in the attempts of the two men to win BIANCA'S attention to themselves as suitors with the waiting one jealously on the watch. In the end, HORTENSIO is not sure about the ' schoolmaster ' CAMBIO, and he concludes the scene with a very firm declaration that he will not be fooled about with, and that if BIANCA wants to, she can become the property of any who wish to have her. All these phases of feeling are roundly modelled and not repressed into too modern a constriction of style.

GLOSSARY OF WORDS

315. Wrangling. 25,4. Disputing, arguing (on some detail or other), the practice of pedants one with the other.

316. Pedant. 25,4. Used contemptuously by Hortensio for ' bookman '. It is adopt. from Fr. *pédant* or its source, It. *pedante* teacher, schoolmaster. Although being used in the more sober meaning, it was often employed to designate inferior theorists and lovers of trifling details.

317. Patroness. 25,5. See note 158. The word in this context means ' one devoted to music because she loves it '.

318. Heavenly harmony. 25,5. ' This is The patroness of heavenly harmony '. Heaven-born music.

319. Prerogative. 25,6. The first turn or preference; adopt. from Fr.-Lat. *praerogātīva* a previous choice or election, preference, privilege.

320. Preposterous. 25,9. Ridiculous; from Lat. meaning ' the putting of the rear to the front '. Lucentio refers to Hortensio's ignorance of the fact that music was given to refresh man after his studies.

321. Usual pain. 25,12. General natural fatigue from various causes.

322. Pause. 25,14. ' While I pause '. While I have a rest after teaching for a time.

323. Braves. 25,15. Affronts.

324. Breeching. 25,18. ' I am no breeching scholar '. Novice; lit. ' one wearing breeches '. A ' breeching ' was a name for flogging, hence a boy still subject to receive the birch.

325. Construe. 25,30. Translate; from Lat. meaning ' to pile together, build up ' also ' to connect grammatically '.

326. Pedascule. 26,6. Tutor (vocative of a coined Lat. ' pedasculus '). The accent is on the second syllable.

327. Æacides. 26,8. The descendants of Æacus, son of Zeus and the nymph Ægina. He was a man of great integrity and grandfather to both Ajax and Achilles.

328. Ajax. 26,9. The bravest of all the Greeks in the Trojan war, and grandson of Æacus.

329. Formal. 26,17. ' Are you so formal, sir ? ' Insistent on formalities, wishing privacy with his pupil.

330. Amorous. 26,19. ' Our fine musician groweth amorous '. He is showing signs of becoming a wooer.

331. Rudiments. 26,22. The first principles; adopt. from Lat. *rudiment -um* beginning, first principles, from *rudis* imperfect.

332. Gamut. 26,23. The ' Great Scale ' comprising the seven hexachords or partial scales, and consisting of all the recognized notes used in medieval music. Lit. it is a contraction of Med. Lat. *gamma ut* from *gamma* (Gk. γ) the initial note in the medieval scale + *ut* the first of a series of six syllables used as the names of the six notes forming a hexachord. See also note 334.

333. Pithy. 26,24. Entertaining because containing substantial fact without etceteras.

334. Re . . . mi . . . fa ut . . . sol . . . la. 26,30-4. The names of the six notes referred to in note 332. They are from the initial syllables of six lines, each of which ascended a degree, in the following Sapphic (the metre used by Sappho and named after her) stanza (Hymn for St John Baptist's Day): *Ut queant laxis resonare fibris Mira gestorum famuli tuorum, Solve polluti labii reatum, Sancte Johannes.*

335. Nice. 26,36. Particular; adopt. from OFr.-Lat. *nescius* ignorant. The word developed many meanings which are too numerous to mention here, and many of them cannot be clearly accounted for. In Shakespeare the usual meaning is that of ' precise ', ' delicate in distinction ' both in pleasant and unpleasant notions.

336. Pry. 26,43. ' I have cause to pry into this pedant ', examine his intentions with closeness.

337. Methinks. 26,44. See note 209.

338. Humble. 26,45. Low in taste.

339. Stale. 26,46. See note 81. Here the meaning is that of ' deceiver '.

340. Ranging. 26,47. Wandering in affection.

341. Changing. 26,48. Reciprocating by seeking some other mistress.

GLOSSARY OF PHRASES

342. Hic ibat Simois; hic est Sigeia tellus; Hic steterat Priami regia celsa senis. 25,28-9. Here ran the river Simois; here is the Sigeian land; here stood the lofty palace of old Priam.

343. Spit in the hole, man, and tune again. 25,38. Lucentio's ridiculing injunction to Hortensio to go away and really tune his instrument.

344. My lessons make no music in three parts. 26,16. His lessons do not require a third part.

345. Call you this gamut ? 26,35. Bianca lays the stress on ' this '. See note 332.

346. Old fashions please me best. 26,36. Bianca prefers the simpler and old-fashioned straightforward method. In other words she is telling Hortensio where he stands in her affection, and that is—not at all.

347. Seize thee that list. 26,47. Let him get you that wants (lusts after) you. ' List ' is from OE. *lystan* to desire.

COMMENTARY

PART I SCENE VII

This is a scene of extravagancies. The situation of PETRUCHIO'S failure to appear is itself under the circumstances a mild absurdity, and so is his appearance later in the eccentric clothing which he has adopted. Hence everything is slightly tinged with over-development without losing natural proportions or becoming farcical. This is the mould in which the scene is cast and it all helps to the principal effect of PETRUCHIO'S bizarre appearance. Thus BAPTISTA is almost on the verge of tears but his feelings are big all the same, and illustrate the calamity of the opening situation. Don't therefore play it in the modern medium because this will not serve any purpose at all. Then we have the forsaken KATHARINA angry and tearful at the same time and rushing off in a torrent of weeping.

Following immediately on this comes the unusual

BIONDELLO who has already been described in Scene III. His treatment must likewise be distinctively curious. He runs in, reeling off his first line in full excitement, and this characterizes his quick cross-talk with the over-wrought BAPTISTA. Then comes his speech with its fantastic details. The pace is fast, but not rushed. Every item must be made clear and an eagerness must characterize the delivery, eagerness to publish this most extraordinary accumulation of oddities such as has never been seen before. It is important to bear this in mind, otherwise the speech becomes a mere rush of words, and it is deprived of its character. There must be definite character in everything that is done in this scene, a basic rationalism in design, a qualifying reason with which there cannot be any conviction. If this is not present *the whole episode will pass for nothing but a superficial imposition on the scene.* BAPTISTA's relief at hearing that, at least, PETRUCHIO is on his way, is as big as he can make it, but it is instantly countered by BIONDELLO's " *Why, sir, he comes not* " made as emphatic as possible to everybody's concern. Then he breaks his joke with hilarity. These details of change awaken the action to its required liveliness.

The whole of the succeeding incident must be played closely by all concerned. BAPTISTA's welcome is truly heartfelt. PETRUCHIO is completely at the top of his form, and BAPTISTA is then as heated as his age and disposition will allow him to be. TRANIO is abrupt with PETRUCHIO in his demand for an explanation of the delay that has made him so late, but he is briefly dismissed by the swift and strenuous bridegroom who proceeds to demand his KATE, as the time is getting on. TRANIO again advances his shocked susceptibilities about PETRUCHIO's unreverent robes. He comes right in on his cue and speaks with urgent force. BAPTISTA almost shrieks out his consternation at the thought of the marriage being celebrated in such attire, but PETRUCHIO is short and peremptory with over-riding maxims and then suddenly recalls the urgency of the moment and goes swiftly off to greet his bride " *And seal the title with lovely kiss* ".

The prime necessity of the scene is a sense of its unorthodox nature, its vitality and widely varied characters each responsible for some quaint change in the action. It is hard-working but methodical and should not be allowed to run riot. *In Shakespeare's work and in every strenuous incident, whether it be in tragedy or comedy, there is always a controlling system of technical direction, and it is this which should first be consulted and instituted as the organizing authority, sober and collected, that teaches the effect to leap and play with meaning.*

GLOSSARY OF WORDS

348. **Rudesby.** 27,10. A character given up entirely to gross behaviour.
349. **Spleen.** 27,10. See note 27.
350. **Passing.** 27,24. See note 212.
351. **Shrew.** 27,29. See note 103.
352. **Thrice turned.** 27,42. ' A pair of breeches thrice turned '. Turned inside out three times, i.e. very old and patched and inside out.
353. **Candle-cases.** 27,43. ' A pair of boots that have been candle-cases '. Used to keep candles in.
354. **Chapeless.** 27,44. Without a chape or metal termination at the extreme point of the scabbard.
355. **Points.** 27,45. The laces used for fastening parts of the dress together, here referring to those supporting the breeches.
356. **Hipped.** 27,45. Lamed in the hip.
357. **Glanders.** 27,46. A contagious disease in horses, the chief symptoms of which are swellings beneath the jaw and discharge of mucous matter from the mouth.
358. **Lampass.** 27,47. A disease incident to horses, consisting in a swelling of the fleshy lining of the roof of the mouth behind the front teeth. The word is usually spelt with only one ' s '.
359. **Windgalls.** 27,48. A soft tumour on either side of a horse's leg just above the fetlock.

360. **Packthread.** 28,7. A coarse thread used for tying up packs or bundles.
361. **Lackey.** 28,9. A footman, especially a running footman; a valet.
362. **Caparisoned.** 28,9. Equipped, decked out.
363. **Stock.** 28,10. Stocking.
364. **Kersey boot-hose.** 28,10. A woollen over-stocking that covered the leg like a jackboot. The material, a cloth made out of long wool, was supposed to have originated at the village of Kersey in Suffolk.
365. **List.** 28,11. ' A red and blue list '. Narrow strips of red and blue cloth.
366. **Monster.** 28,12. See note 14.
367. **Humour.** 28,14. ' Some odd humour '. Some freakish whim. See note 36.
368. **But.** 28,15. ' He goes but mean-apparell'd '. Only in mean clothes. ' But ' is from OE. *be-ūtan, būtan, būta* on the outside, without. From this arises the exceptive sense of the word in a variety of forms, ' only ' being one, as here.
369. **Jamy.** 28,23. ' Saint Jamy '. Saint James.
370. **Hold.** 28,24. Wager. Lit. money held in the hand as a wager.
371. **Gallants.** 28,28. ' Where be these gallants ? ' Finely-dressed people.

The accent is on the second syllable. Petruchio is drawing a contrast between them and himself.
372. **Halt.** 28,31. See note 245. Baptista observes this after Petruchio's assertion that he comes not well, taking it in the sense that he does not show lameness in his rush into the room.
373. **Better.** 28,34. Accent this word so as to clear the meaning of the line. ' Even if he were better dressed he would rush in just the same '.
374. **Monument.** 28,38. Manifestation.
375. **Prodigy.** 28,39. Something extraordinary from which an omen can be drawn; something causing wonder. It comes from Lat. meaning ' something which speaks before '.
376. **Unprovided.** 28,42. ' You come so unprovided '. Unsuitably attired. Baptista is alluding to Petruchio's eccentric clothes.
377. **Estate.** 28,43. Rank (as a gentleman).
378. **Tedious.** 28,48. Lit. irksome; from Lat. *taedium.*
379. **Accoutrements.** 29,9. Clothes other than the ordinary. Of uncertain origin; probably from Fr. *à* to + *cous-tre, coutre* a sacristan who robed the clergyman.
380. **Event.** 29,17. Issue, result.

GLOSSARY OF PHRASES

381. **Hiding his bitter jests in blunt behaviour.** 27,13. Assuming his unmannerly conduct in order to practise jests which bite with deep insult.
382. **Stirrups of no kindred.** 27,46. Neither stirrup matching the other either in shape or size.

383. **To mose in the chine.** 27,47. ' Mourning of the chine ' is a disorder in horses. The ' chine ' is the backbone.
384. **Infected with the fashions.** 27,47-8. Infected with farcin (of which ' fashions ' is an obsolete variation), a disease of horses closely allied to glanders.

385. **Sped with spavins.** 27,48. Completely done for owing to a disease causing swelling of the joints.
386. **Rayed with the yellows.** 27,48. Defiled with jaundice. ' To ray ' is an aphetic form of the verb ' to array ', to arrange, order, equip. It came to be used in specific contexts to mean ' to dirty, soil, spoil, befoul '.
387. **Past cure of the fives.** 28,1. Beyond curing of the ' vives ', aphetic form of ' avives ', a disease of the salivary glands in young horses.
388. **Stark spoiled with the staggers.** 28,1. Completely victimized with a disease in young cattle that causes giddiness.
389. **Begnawn with the bots.** 28,1-2. Eaten up with a disease of horses caused by parasitic worms or maggots.
390. **Swayed in the back and shoulder-shotten.** 28,2. Sunk in the backbone and the shoulders dislocated or strained. ' Shotten ' is a participial adjective meaning ' shot ' or exhausted, the strength abstracted.
391. **Near-legged before.** 28,2. Going with the fore-legs close together.

392. **A half-checked (cheeked) bit.** 28,3. Said of a bit in which the bridle is attached half-way up the cheek or side-piece, thus giving insufficient control over the horse's mouth--C. T. Onions.
393. **Head-stall of sheep's leather.** 28,3. The part of the bridle that fits round the head.
394. **One girth six times pieced.** 28,5. The girth that holds the saddle on to the horse's body is in six pieces.
395. **Crupper of velure.** 28,6. The strap that keeps the saddle in position by passing under the tail. This one is of velvet.
396. **Fairly set down in studs.** 28,6-7. Embossed, raised up attractively in some system of relief.
397. *The humour of forty fancies* **pricked in't.** 28,11-12. Conjectured to be an old ballad, probably a love-ballad. It is fastened to Petruchio's hat with a pin.
398. **And yet I come not well.** 28,30. And yet he comes not in an agreeable or acceptable way.
399. **Though in some part enforced to digress.** 28,50. Petruchio has had to give his attention for a while to other things, to go aside away from his main purpose.

COMMENTARY

PART I   SCENE VIII

After the highly charged action of the scene which has just finished, a slight rest is needed. We have a further scene of similar pitch to follow and so an easing is used to prepare the mind for further intensive interest. This scene therefore is necessary and welcome, but at the same time it must have an activity of its own, for rest is not idleness, but change of occupation. Thought and interest must work and be kept alert for further change. Thus the opening dialogue to this scene must be earnest and the matter made important because it is plot and concerns the successful issue of LUCENTIO's romance. Therefore keep the pace fairly fast and the details developed with eagerness and not just discussed. By this means a common nature is sustained between this scene and its two neighbours, and there is no undue pause. Of course, there is nothing boisterous about the treatment. We have had enough of that and it would only be objectionable in more ways than one : but intense activity of an intimate kind is necessary here.

After the little introductory passage, GREMIO appears and creates an entirely new atmosphere. His character is used very profitably. He is not a man who can hurry, but must take his time over details, and in doing so he makes them interesting. As he arrives, we realize that he has seen something extraordinary. He can only declare himself in the strongest terms. In his speech he is highly graphic, and dramatizes the events related with vivid attention to detail. The scene, therefore, is alive with action, less energetic than that which qualifies its companions, but serving its purpose in this very way.

GLOSSARY OF WORDS

400. **Skills.** 29,22. ' It skills not much '. it makes no difference; adopt. from O.Norse *skilja* to divide, distinguish, etc., or *skila* to decide, expound.
401. **Turn.** 29,22. Requirements.
402. **Make assurance.** 29,24. Given [a written guarantee. See note 283.
403. **Consent.** 29,27. ' With consent '. i.e. with the consent of Bianca's father.
404. **Methinks.** 29,30. See note 209.
405. **Steal.** 29,30. ' To steal our marriage '. To marry secretly, without Baptista's knowledge or consent.
406. **Vantage.** 29,34. ' And watch our vantage in this business '. Opportunities. Tranio is going to keep his eyes open for any opportunity by means of

which Bianca and Lucentio can achieve a secret marriage.
407. **Narrow-prying.** 29,36. See note 336.
408. **Quaint.** 29,37. Knowing, clever, crafty; adopt. from OFr. *cointe, queinte*-Lat. *cognitum* known. Thus the meaning came to be applied to things of ingenious quality or design.
409. **Amorous.** 29,37. See note 330.
410. **Groom.** 29,42. ' 'Tis a groom indeed '. Using the language and behaviour of a serving-man. The word until the 17th c. only had the meaning of ' horse-groom ' by context that directly named the groom as such.
411. **Gogs-wouns.** 30,1. God's wounds.
412. **List.** 30,6. See note 347.
413. **Cozen.** 30,9. Deceive. Explained

by Cotgrove (1611) as originating from the practice of travellers claiming kindred in order to secure free lodging.
414. **Carousing.** 30,12. See note 183.
415. **Muscadel.** 30,13. A strong sweet wine made of the muscat or similar grape.
416. **Sops.** 30,14. Cakes or wafers put into a drink to float on top.
417. **Parting.** 30,20. As the lips were drawn apart.
418. **Rout.** 30,22. ' After me, I know, the rout is coming '. The company, the wedding-party and guests; adopt. through AFr. and OFr. from Lat. *rupta* fem. of *rup'us* broken, the original sense being ' division, detachment '.

COMMENTARY

PART I   SCENE IX

Now we come back to action of the more intensive kind, spirited, forceful and fast. PETRUCHIO is exuberance itself, but in the first part of the scene he is happy, conversational in style, collo-quial although virile. He does not waste any time over what he says, but is politely definite throughout. Don't just rush through his first two speeches but let us realize what he is talking about.

When entreated by TRANIO and GREMIO each retort is immediate and courteously definite. Then there is a slight pause ; and in contrast to the urgency of the other two, KATHARINA comes to PETRUCHIO, takes her time, and then entreats him with a strength, suppressed and measured. This treatment by its complete variation gives it emphasis, especially as it is the first time that KATHARINA shows the evidence of bending (if somewhat forced) spirit.

PETRUCHIO answers perfectly easily and with pleasant emphasis. KATHARINA then bursts out with greater feeling to which PETRUCHIO (highly amused) replies with a sharp order given to GRUMIO, making a pause after " Grumio ", and, still looking steadily at KATHARINA, then completes the adversative reply. After GRUMIO's quick, inverted acknowledgment, KATHARINA asserts herself without any mistake. Then she takes the stage with complete authority and dignity and instructs everyone to go forward to the bridal dinner. At this, PETRUCHIO takes command again with jovial and forceful support of KATHARINA's invitation, suddenly showing his own intention to go off and take KATE with him. Then he asserts a forcefully commanding strength over

the situation, which he works up to a fantastic, but artistically *designed* climax, all, of course, the work of his exuberant spirits, and every moment one of delight to himself. Once again, let us remind the reader that the treatment must respect the action and not spend itself in unintelligent or uncontrolled haste. The points which have been enumerated will help to advertise what is required. In the final speech, " *But for my bonny Kate, she must with me* ", is slower, more emphatic. It is the determining line in the speech. The next five lines are faster, but the words and the sense must be respected. " *And here she stands, touch her whoever dare* " is again a superior line, strong and challenging, and requiring specific attention, but not delaying the general movement of the speech.

As has already been said, the whole substance of the scene as far as PETRUCHIO is concerned springs from a handling of the situation without any ostentatious strength until the final speech. There is purpose behind his seeming irresponsibility, and everything that he says and does is managed and is not just emptily free and easy. But a great sense of humour also predominates. How else could the final episode be achieved ?

GLOSSARY OF WORDS

419. **Jolly.** 31,7. Insolent, overbearing. It is one of the early variations of the meaning of the word whose fundamental signification is ' lively, gay, festive ', etc. Perhaps being over-jolly may lead to pride, insolence, etc., from which the textual meaning originated.
420. **Groom.** 31,7. Bridegroom.
421. **Domineer.** 31,18. Revel, feast

riotously; apparently adopt. from early modern Dutch *dominer-en* to rule, have dominion. The present meaning is from *domineren* to feast luxuriously, probably like lords or rulers. Is now obsolete.

422. **Carouse.** 31,19. See note 183.
423. **Maidenhead.** 31,19. Virgin state.

424. **Fret.** 31,22. See note 220.
425. **Chattels.** 31,24. Moveable possessions; adopt. from OFr.-Lat. meaning ' principal, property, goods ' etc.
426. **Household stuff.** 31,25. See note 61.
427. **He.** 31,28. ' The proudest he '. The personal pronoun used instead of ' man ' or similar noun.

GLOSSARY OF PHRASES

428. **You may be jogging whiles your boots are green.** 31,5. Petruchio can go off if he wants to; he can go plodding on as long as he has leather to the soles of his boots.

429. **That take it on you at the first so roundly.** 31,8. Who adopts this bald behaviour.
430. **Go hang yourselves.** 31,20. Do whatever you like.
431. **I'll bring mine action.** 31,28. i.e. legal action.

COMMENTARY

PART I SCENE X

If this short scene is kept in, make it lively ; but, unless a full version is being presented, the

first half of the play should end after the preceding scene.

GLOSSARY OF WORDS

432. **Kated.** 31,39. ' Petruchio is Kated '. Catted, provided with a cat. See note 191.

433. **Wants.** 31,41. ' Though bride and bridegroom wants '. Lacks. Bride and groom are taken as one quantity.

434. **Junkets.** 31,43. Delicacies, dainty appetizing foods. The history of the word is somewhat obscure.

COMMENTARY

PART II SCENE I

The opening of this scene can be dull unless great pains are taken to make it otherwise. It is not akin to what has gone before in liveliness of nature, neither does the humour scintillate. GRUMIO is tired, distressed and cold. He is an indication of the woes that have been attending the journey to the house. He cannot be expected to revel in sparkling humour, but he must exercise his opportunities in their own peculiar capacities. Although tired out, keep him mindful of his own discomforts but not too slow in delivery. His troubles are real to him, and to hear them feelingly told gives us an overture to what is to come. CURTIS, of course, is lively and cheerful. He has not been out on a journey. GRUMIO quickens appreciably on " Where's the cook . . . ? " this being a sudden recollection of essential requirements. Then he proceeds to tell his story in precise detail interrupted first by a little playful knock-about comedy, and then by a spasm of temperament. " Tell thou the tale " is a decided snap at CURTIS. Then he proceeds to tell his story ' temperamentally ', and at the same time very colourfully, ending with a bitter sting and hoping it will hurt. Then he suddenly recollects the approach of his master and mistress and becomes vigorously concerned about the servants. His cross-talk with CURTIS which follows this (if kept in) is quick. Then the Servants enter with a very warm greeting for GRUMIO which is interrupted by the arrival of PETRUCHIO and KATHARINA.

PETRUCHIO opens the scene with dominant style. Poor GRUMIO rattles off his speech of excuses in fear of his life. The whole atmosphere of the following episode up until the exit of PETRUCHIO and KATHARINA must be that of complete disorder and frustration designed to confuse KATHARINA in every way possible. Throughout the action, PETRUCHIO's humour asserts itself all the time. He is thoroughly enjoying the whole affair and, of course, assumes every variation with deliberate design. This enables him to obtain changes with clear-cut suddenness. After singing " Where is the life . . . ? " he suddenly roars out " Where are those——", and then breaks off to bid KATE be merry, with bright affability. The similar changes that plainly occur in the next few lines should show this facility of purposed manoeuvring which provides great entertainment as well as action. To maintain a consistent sternness or noisiness is bad art and nothing of any real value or attractive effect comes from such treatment. KATHARINA's individuality in its severity of nature

must be kept singular. PETRUCHIO must break his lines up into their separate sentiments, so as to establish their definite natures and then apply the treatment so that it achieves an easy transposition from one effect to the other. Don't row all the time. It gets tiring and ineffectual. " Get water, here, what, ho ! " and " Shall I have some water " are bellowed out, but the intervening phrases are lively in various other ways. " Come, KATE, and wash . . ." is sweetly polite. Also in his next speech, PETRUCHIO roundly abuses the " flap-eared knave " and then turns to his wife with all the sweetness in the world just as though they were about to have a happy and quiet little meal together. Then " What's this ? Mutton ? " begins a development that commences with (purposed) astonishment at the condition of the meat. " Who bought it ? " promises great trouble for the one concerned, not through shouting, but ominous intensity, that explodes in " 'Tis burnt " and takes a drastic course until the ' joltheads ' are driven from the stage under the missiles of the meal itself and the utensils. Then he turns to KATHARINA, who for the second time tries to be pacifying, and this, on her part, is a genuine attempt made strenuously but as an appeal. He addresses her with the most careful and precise explanation of the reason why the meal was so unfit. This is said with the utmost consideration and affability. This heightens the irony of the last two lines of the speech, which are taken with even greater gentleness still.

The Servants must supply their commentary with intensive emphasis, because they are indicating the situation. " He kills her in her own humour " is the summary of the entire action of the play, and is announced as a real, important fact ; and CURTIS just makes the events he describes as graphic as possible. PETRUCHIO in his final speech is, of course, perfectly normal.

The whole scene is slightly fantasticated, but without losing any natural proportions. It requires preconceived planning and judicious handling of the more noisy parts so that they are governed by proper modification of their environing phrases. PETRUCHIO, as has already been pointed out, must arrange everything he says for deliberate effect and with a keen humour seasoning his administration of that effect. Gentleness and violence work side by side, and exaggeration is offset by its obviously ridiculous circumstances. But it still requires art and control to give it proper shape and dramatic conviction.

GLOSSARY OF WORDS

435. **Jades.** 32,1. See note 174.
436. **Rayed.** 32,2. See note 386.
437. **Taller.** 32,8. Worthier, hardier. The word ' tall ' was frequently used in the sense of ' character, spirit, quality of bearing '.
438. **Shrew.** 32,16. See note 103.
439. **Tames.** 32,18. Quietens the sexual impulse.
440. **Coney-catching.** 32,30. Rabbit-catching; formerly the proper and ordinary name, but now superseded in general use by ' rabbit ', which was originally a name for the young only. This present phrase was used to mean ' cheating, duping, knavery ', i.e. catching out by a trick or trap, as when snaring conies. Curtis probably uses the word to mean that he is fond of telling ' fairy-tales ' for news, cheating by invention.
441. **Rushes.** 32,32. ' Rushes strewed '. Rushes were strewn on the floor.
442. **Fustian.** 32,33. A kind of coarse cloth made of cotton and flax.
443. **Officer.** 32,34. The heads of all the household departments.
444. **Carpets.** 32,35. Carpets were used in certain rooms of the house. They were also used to cover beds and tables.
445. **Sensible.** 32,48. ' A sensible tale '. A play upon the double meaning of the word: (a) sensible, (b) felt, because Grumio has struck Curtis' ear when asking him to ' lend it ' to him.
446. **Imprimis.** 33,1. In the first place.
447. **Bemoiled.** 33,8. Wet and muddy.
448. **Crupper.** 33,12. See note 395.
449. **Indifferent.** 33,20. See note 164.

450. **Countenance.** 33,25-6. ' To countenance my mistress '. To honour her, give her the ceremonial attendance which is due to her as their mistress. ' To give countenance ' to anything was to look upon it with favour, give it authority and position. Curtis does later explain himself in these terms. See also note 114.
451. **Countenance.** 33,29. ' Company to countenance her '. Grumio deliberately misinterprets Curtis' meaning and applies that of ' face ', purely and simply. See also note 114.
452. **Spruce.** 33,39. Smart in appearance.
453. **Neat.** 33,40. ' All things neat '. Just where they should be.
454. **Cock's passion.** 33,43. God's Passion.
455. **Logger-headed.** 33,49. Wooden-headed.
456. **Unpolish'd.** 33,49. Uncouth.
457. **Peasant swain.** 34,1. A duplication of the same epithet for emphasis.
458. **Whoreson.** 34,1. Son of a whore, simply an abusive name.
459. **Malt-horse.** 34,1. A term of abuse implying that Grumio is simply a slow, unimaginative creature, heavy-going in mind and body as a beast of burden. The word ' drudge ' is included in this meaning.
460. **Pumps.** 34,6. Close-fitting slippers without fasteners over the instep. The origin of the word is unknown.
461. **Unpink'd.** 34,6. Without any eyelet holes in the heels for laces to go through.
462. **Link.** 34,7. Lamp-black, made from links or torches.

463. **Soud.** 34,15. This is simply an expression of exhaustion or being overheated.
464. **Mend.** 34,21. ' Mend the plucking off the other '. Take more care in plucking off the other boot.
465. **Beetle-headed.** 34,30. Thick-headed; probably derived from the heavy type of wooden hammer, known as a beetle, requiring three men to lift it.
466. **Flap-ear'd.** 34,30. Probably with reference to the large, flapping ears on a fool's cap, and so likening him to the wearer.
467. **Trenchers.** 34,41. Round or square pieces of wood on which meat was served and cut up. It comes from Fr. meaning ' to cut '.
468. **Joltheads.** 34,42. Blockheads. The origin of the word is unknown.
469. **Grumble.** 34,43. Utter meaningless, inarticulate sounds.
470. **Choler.** 34,48. One of the four fluids causing the ' humours ', in this case that of anger. See note 36.
471. **Continency.** 35,9. Self-restraint in sexual passion.
472. **Rails.** 35,11. See note 52.
473. **Rates.** 35,11. ' And rails, and swears, and rates '. Verbally ' tearing her to pieces '. It has a stronger action than ' rails ' and suggests more closely analytical terms. Its origin is unknown.
474. **Kites.** 35,22. Birds of prey of the falcon family.
475. **Bate and beat.** 35,23. Beat the wings impatiently and flutter away from the fist or perch.
476. **Hurly.** 35,30. Uproar and strife.

GLOSSARY OF PHRASES

477. **Cast on no water.** 32,14-15. ' Scotland burneth, Scotland burneth—Fire, fire:—Fire, fire, Cast on some more water '. From an old ballad, quoted by Blackstone—Arden Edition Shakespeare.
478. **Do thy duty, and have thy duty.** 32,25. Perform the duty of fire-making, and enjoy what has been done.
479. **Jack, boy ! ho ! boy !** 32,28. The beginning of an old round in three parts.
480. **And as much news as will thaw.** 32,28-9. As much as the warmth of the fire will cause Grumio to remember.
481. **Be the jacks fair within, the jills fair without.** 32,34-5. The men-servants and maid-servants, the first in the kitchen (within) being trim and the second being fair in appearance.
482. **Why, a horse.** 33,5. One horse the less to be cleaned and looked after. Grumio says that Petruchio was riding down a foul hill behind Katharina. Curtis asks if they were both on the one horse; and Grumio asks what that should mean to Curtis.
483. **Till they kiss their hands.** 33,21-2. It was a common

courtesy to kiss one's own hand out of respect to another person, and was practised at court.
484. **He kills her in her own humour.** 35,7. He kills her humour by adopting the same humour in himself. For ' humour ' see note 36.
485. **My falcon now is sharp and passing empty.** 35,17. In falconry, the hawk is kept from food prior to being used for hunting. ' Sharp ' = keen with appetite.
486. **And till she stoop she must not be full-gorged.** 35,18. ' Stoop ' signifies ' when a Hawke being upon her wings at the height of her pitch, bendeth violentlie downe to strike the fowle or other prey '—Latham, 1615. Petruchio is referring to Katharina as to a hawk being submitted to discipline in order to bring her into useful tameness.
487. **For then she never looks upon her lure.** 35,19. If she is gorged with food, she will not attack her prey.
488. **Man my haggard.** 35,20. Accustom the hawk to the presence of men. ' Haggard ' = a wild (female) hawk caught when in her adult plumage. From this comes the more familiar meaning of the word, ' wild, worn, distressed-looking '.

COMMENTARY

PART II SCENE II

The scene must open vigorously. TRANIO, like PETRUCHIO, is playing a part, and a suspicion of BIANCA's possible infidelity towards him is met with a deliberately pointed rejoinder from HORTENSIO ; and after the short appearance of LUCENTIO and BIANCA, the whole passage is treated with slight over-intensity. HORTENSIO is an innocent victim of a trick in which TRANIO is one of the originators. The consternation of the latter at BIANCA's behaviour with LUCENTIO is purposely enlarged in order to incite HORTENSIO's

resentment against BIANCA and so secure his withdrawal from the suit. Both men in this passage must therefore intensify their treatment. HORTENSIO's reactions must likewise respond to those of TRANIO in equal breadth and thus we get vitality and that slight abnormality of treatment that belongs to this play. To have it in one scene and to lose it in another, even though the actual character of the action is not so vigorous, will give an unevenness to the general effect, and make the more powerful incidents seem to overbalance the rest. It will always be found, either in the dialogue or other form of construction. The treatment does not drop to purely modern conversational level. There is always a fullness, ripeness and sense of power however slender the passage.

Thus, after HORTENSIO has left the scene, there is a spirit of glee among the three characters concerned. HORTENSIO has been disposed of, and the consequent elation of feeling animates the action. "*And I have forsworn you with Hortensio*" is said with mock formality, slightly and laughingly exaggerated. BIANCA's question tinkles with humour and TRANIO replies with the same mock style as before accompanied by an elaborate bow. LUCENTIO comes in quickly and eagerly with "*Then we are rid of Licio*". Thus this little episode proceeds to its close without dropping its pitch. Play quickly but make all the points.

BIONDELLO then enters with news of a development. He alters the treatment and gives a change by telling us, in his own drawn-out way, of his weariness. Then he announces the reward of his watching, the "*ancient angel coming down the hill*", one sent as an answer to their needs, and hands out the required details in one last effort for their satisfaction. TRANIO transmits this favour of fortune to LUCENTIO in rapid but emphatic explanation and then swiftly dismisses him and his sweetheart.

In the PEDANT, we have an innocent old gentleman being moulded into a false situation by the energetic TRANIO. Here again we require an agile inventing and then the applying of facts for all they are worth. The PEDANT responds with complete ease to TRANIO's terrifying news and soon becomes involved in his wiles. The threat to his life, so forcibly revealed by TRANIO, dissolves him in a cry of terror : "*My life, sir ! how, I pray ?*", and he is instantly taken in hand by the other and left without any shadow of a doubt about his great danger. Then TRANIO, with the ostensible purpose of saving the PEDANT's life, very graciously, but also with careful pointedness, offers him a favour which the old man accepts with the deepest gratitude, and receives a further piece of information to be made clearer as he goes off to TRANIO's lodging.

The whole scene requires to be handled with appropriate virility and each episode dealt with in the full manner that has been indicated.

GLOSSARY OF WORDS

489. Fair in hand. 35,41. 'She bears me fair in hand'. Tranio asserts that Bianca is faithful to him and has no interest in anyone else.

490. Quick proceeders. 36,6. Quick workers.

491. Wonderful. 36,10. Past belief, in a deprecatory sense.

492. Cullion. 36,15. A vile fellow. The word is adopt. from Fr. meaning ' bag, testicle '.

493. Lightness. 36,19. Lightness of character, infidelity.

494. Forswear. 36,24. Renounce, abjure: lit. ' away swear ' ' depart from the oath '.

495. Beastly. 36,29. 'How beastly she doth court him '. Heatedly, without maidenly restraint. This is probably an exaggeration on Tranio's part in order to effect Hortensio's complete renunciation of Bianca.

496. Haggard. 36,34. See note 488.

497. Napping. 36,41. Off her guard.

498. Lusty. 36,46. See note 224.

499. Dog-weary. 37,5. Dog-tired, like a dog wearied after a long chase.

500. Angel. 37,6. ' An ancient angel '. ' A fellow of th'old sound, honest and worthie stampe ' — Cotgrave. An ' angel ' was a gold coin having the figure of St Michael as its device, and valued at from 6s. 8d. to 10s. according to the period. Hence the present pun.

501. Mercatante. 37,9. From It. meaning ' merchant '.

502. Pedant. 37,9. See note 316.

503. Formal. 37,10. ' Formal in apparel '. Distinct in his dress as belonging to a certain class such as either of those just mentioned.

504. Gait. 37,11. Manner of walking.

505. Countenance. 37,11. See note 114. Here it means ' bearing '; he carries himself like an elderly man.

506. Credulous. 37,13. Easily believing, capable of being imposed upon. It is from Lat. meaning ' ready or disposed to believe '.

507. Credit. 38,3. Honourable condition.

508. Repute. 38,9. Reckon, esteem.

509. Dower. 38,14. See note 94.

GLOSSARY OF PHRASES

510. That teacheth tricks eleven and twenty long, To tame a shrew and charm her chattering tongue. 37,2–3. This obviously refers to some proverbial saying that cannot be traced.

COMMENTARY

PART II SCENE III

Shakespeare knew how to preserve his values. In the former scene with KATHARINA there was a good deal of rough and tumble and full-voiced strength. That is done with. To attempt to use that style any further would ruin the artistry of the work. Hence in the main, any open vigour of action is confined to certain specific points, and PETRUCHIO is scarcely concerned with them. It is an illustration of that prevailing method in Shakespeare's work—and we have referred to it before—the inevitable artist that subdues all things to governed form and function irrespective of its dramatic nature.

PETRUCHIO throughout this scene plays very colloquially. Examine the lines and you will see how effective they are when dealt with in this way, especially after the full volume of his previous scene. It also keeps his charm before us, and eliminates anything of the bully, and so makes the play more pleasant than it would be otherwise.

F

Before proceeding any further with the main part of the scene, let us briefly examine the earlier part, the passage between KATHARINA and CURTIS. KATHARINA is on the point of tears, bitter tears, and her speech shows that she is breaking under the strain. GRUMIO, obviously acting under PETRUCHIO's orders, tantalizes her, by suggesting the most appetizing dishes in a most appetizing way, only to withdraw them under the pretext that they feed temper as well. He does this artfully and leads poor KATHARINA into greater pangs. Don't just be straightforward but nurse the treatment in order to do this. Then finally he becomes downright in his annoying word-play and this drives KATHARINA into a frenzy which is stopped by the appearance of PETRUCHIO and HORTENSIO.

Her husband addresses her quite amiably. His enquiry is perfectly light and so is his following speech, no labouring of points or driving home of comments. Taken in this way as against her bitter resentment and aggressiveness, makes the situation more effective. It is designed triviality on PETRUCHIO's part. One can almost hear him say " Dear, dear, dear ". In dealing thus with the treatment, do not throw the lines away. Although seemingly matter of fact, there is purpose in what he is doing, and his voice is modulated to express this. KATHARINA, after a pause, suddenly blurts out " I pray you, let it stand ", to which PETRUCHIO immediately replies in his same easy, but meaning way. Contrast of treatment reserves the particular quality of each character to itself, avoids sameness and heightens the effect of each.

Once served with a mite of food, KATHARINA quickly eats it whilst PETRUCHIO rattles off his long speech with bright spirit as though everybody were perfectly happy, KATHARINA included. Then suddenly seeing her empty plate, he says quite lightly " What, hast thou dined ? " ignoring the fact that hardly anything had been given her to eat. Then immediately after, the TAILOR appears, and PETRUCHIO turns happily and at once to him with glad anticipation of all the nice dresses that he has doubtless brought with him. He adroitly perches the cap brought by the haberdasher on his finger and criticizes it in an easy colloquial way, but also with emphasis. Don't eliminate the character of the passage by too trivial a treatment but give it its point. The easy style offers a contrast to KATHARINA who can assert herself without having to over-act. PETRU-

CHIO's reply to her comment is pointed but polite, quite delightful and without any aggressiveness. KATHARINA then expresses herself in strong terms to which PETRUCHIO listens with perfect patience and amusement, and then with the same easy treatment as before just makes her look foolish by pleasantly assuming that she has been angry against the cap.

In the succeeding scene with the TAILOR, PETRUCHIO is deliberately critical but still uses a colloquial treatment. The effect is much better than over-weighted violence, and gives PETRUCHIO an attractive strength. We must keep that quality always in view.

The scene between GRUMIO and the TAILOR is a lively little development that takes the interest upon itself for the time being, gives us an amusing change and spaces out the scene between its main objectives so as to relieve them as well as prevent too abrupt a succession. It provides a contest between two entirely different characters, with the spirited little TAILOR bravely holding his own and GRUMIO finding himself losing ground until he seizes on a quibble and strenuously grapples with his undaunted opponent both verbally and physically. It is better to omit the text after " Spare not me ". After GRUMIO has beaten the TAILOR out, jump to PETRUCHIO's line " Hortensio, say thou wilt see the Tailor paid ", on which HORTENSIO exits. Then PETRUCHIO turns to KATHARINA and resumes the scene with her.

His speech is again pleasant, warm-hearted, gentle and pointed in a colloquial way. Nothing is laboured, and yet all the details are treated with consideration and feeling. KATHARINA, however, picks up PETRUCHIO's deliberate miscalculations and bitterly exclaims against them, at which he responds with definite assertiveness but without undue force. He continues in the same manner, and then goes to the door, calls out to his men his determination not to travel, and then with polite pointedness makes it plainly evident that things are going to be done according to his will.

It will be seen that there is a delicacy at work within the framework of this scene as well as in the others, that balances characters and effects and so gives the product the unique quality common to all the Poet's writings. It is a great pity that this singular qualification is not more studied and observed. The results would be so much more enlightening.

GLOSSARY OF WORDS

511. **Present alms.** 38,22. Immediate satisfaction.
512. **Spites.** 38,28. Teases. It is not so much the wants and their denial which are exasperating to Katharina, but the fact that Petruchio pretends that he

fears that death may lurk in gratifying her wants which adds to the greater teasing nature of his behaviour.
513. **Neat.** 38,34. An animal of the ox-kind.
514. **Passing.** 38,35. See note 212.

515. **Choleric.** 38,36. See notes 36 and 470.
516. **False deluding.** 39,3. An instance of a compound wherein the first word is Anglo-Saxon and denotes the notion and the second word is of classical

530. **Masquing stuff.** 40,15. Fantastic clothes such as were used in masques.

531. **Demi-cannon.** 40,16. A kind of a large gun formerly used, of about 6½ inches bore. It was about half the size of the usual variety of cannon.

532. **Kennel.** 40,26. ' Hop me over every kennel home '. Hop over every drain, the kennel being the open drain in the street. It is a later form of ME. *Canel*, *Kanel*, adopt. from O.Norm.F. *Canel*, Channel of a river; the central OFr. form was Chanel whence the parallel ME. *Chanel*, later *Channel*.

533. **Commendable.** 40,30. The accent is on the first syllable. This is the Shakespearean use.

534. **Puppet.** 40,31. ' You mean to make a puppet of me '. Dressed up like a doll. In the following two lines the word is purposely used in a more contemptuous signification; for a woman to be called a puppet was anything but pleasant.

535. **Monstrous.** 40,34. See note 14.

536. **Nail.** 40,36. A measure of length for cloth. It equals 2¼ inches or the sixteenth part of a yard.

537. **Winter-cricket.** 40,37. Probably because of his thin, chirpy voice.

538. **Quantity.** 40,39. Diminutive portion.

539. **Be-mete.** 40,40. Measure, by applying the measuring-yard in the form of blows. ' Mete ' is from OE. meaning ' to measure '.

540. **Yard.** 40,40. Mete-yard, measuring rod or stick; OE. *ʒyrd*, *ʒird* a stick, rod.

541. **Prating.** 40,41. Talking in an irresponsible, meaningless way.

542. **Ergo.** 40,54. Lat. therefore.

543. **Note.** 40,56. ' Note of the fashion '. The written authorization for the

---

517. **Sweeting.** 39,8. A noun of great endearment: lit. ' born of sweetness '.

518. **Amort.** 39,8. Put out; lit. in a condition of death.

519. **Ruffs.** 39,30. The pleated, starched collars worn alike by men and women and made of cambric, lawn, holland or other fine cloth.

520. **Fardingales.** 39,30. The more usual spelling is ' farthingales '. A skirt laid over a series of hoops so that it stands out from the body; adapt. from OFr. *verdugale*, *vertugalle* a corruption of Sp. *verdugado* a farthingale, from *verdugo* rod, stick (so-called because the skirt is distended by cane hoops or rods inserted underneath).

521. **Knavery.** 39,32. Things of cunning nature and show, a meaning now obsolete.

522. **Ruffling.** 39,34. Dresses plenteous with ruffles or frills.

523. **Porringer.** 39,39. A small bowl for porridge.

524. **Dish.** 39,40. i.e. the cap is shaped like a dish.

525. **Lewd.** 39,40. Debased in design and taste.

526. **Paltry.** 40,9. Trashy, worthless.

527. **Coffin.** 40,10. ' A custard coffin '. Crust of a custard.

528. **Bauble.** 40,10. A piece of finery and nothing more.

529. **Silken pie.** 40,10. A pie-dish made of silk.

---

origin describing the action of the first. Shakespeare uses this quite frequently. It gives a complete and therefore more intensive nature to the utterance. ' False ' = wrong, contrary to what is true; ' deluding ' means ' playing or acting false, making game of '; *de* put down or subject to some indignity + *ludere* to play.

---

garment to be made in the fashionable style.

544. **Imprimis.** 41,3. Lat. in the first place.

545. **Bottom.** 41,5. ' A bottom of brown thread '. A skein or ball of brown thread, probably derived from the foundation or bottom roll upon which the rest is wound.

546. **Compassed cape.** 41,8. A cape that opens in the front like an inverted V, ' compass-wise ' as Hall calls it, according to Planché, because the appearance is that of a pair of compasses. The usual definition is ' circular ', but is any cloak made otherwise ?

547. **Trunk sleeve.** 41,10. A sleeve large and wide in the upper part.

548. **Curiously.** 41,12. ' The sleeves curiously cut '. Fastidiously; adopt. from OFr.-Lat. meaning ' full of care or pains, careful, inquisitive '.

549. **Conceit.** 41,28. ' What's your conceit in that ? ' Meaning, the substantial thought behind it; Lat. *conceptus* a conceiving. Petruchio asks Grumio just what he understands in the phrase ' take it up '.

550. **Habiliments.** 41,38. Furnishings, full requirements of equipment or clothing for some particular purpose. Thus this is a rather jocular allusion to their ' mean ' garments ; adopt. from OFr. meaning ' to render fit, fit out ' from *habile* fit, suitable.

551. **Jay.** 41,43. A bird resembling a magpie and having plumage or striking appearance.

552. **Furniture.** 41,48. Clothing, another somewhat jocular elaboration of the real condition of Katharina's poor attire.

553. **Frolic.** 41,50. Make merry. The noun is derived from this verb.

554. **Gallant.** 42,8. The accent is on the first syllable, for scansion.

GLOSSARY OF PHRASES

555. **The more my wrong, the more his spite appears.** 38,19. The more Katharina's shrewishness asserts itself . . .

556. **That feed'st me with the very name of meat.** 39,4. Katharina abuses Grumio because he only feeds her bitterness and the acuteness of her starvation with the very name of meat.

557. **Sorted to no proof.** 39,16. Petruchio observes that all the trouble that he has gone to to provide appetizing food for Katharina (after taking it away because she will not say thank you) does not meet with any proof that she needs it.

558. **Double change of bravery.** 39,31. A variety of ornaments and luxuries.

559. **A knack, a toy, a trick, a baby's cap.** 39,42. They all mean the same thing, something to amuse children by its fanciful, toy-like nature.

560. **I love thee well, in that thou likest it not.** 40,11. Petruchio admires Katharina because she has no taste for the cap, completely ignoring the fact that it attracts her.

561. **Carved like an apple-tart.** 40,17. Cut with openings, an allusion to the prevailing fashion of ' slashed ' sleeves with the lining protruding through the slashings.

562. **A censer in a barber's shop.** 40,19. Censers, vessels containing burning charcoal, were used to fumigate rooms with perfume, and were to be found in barbers' shops.

563. **As thou shalt think on prating whilst thou livest.** 40,41. Petruchio threatens to cause the Tailor to have reason never to forget the foolishness of prating.

564. **The sleeves should be cut out and sewed up again.** 41,14-15. Cut out of the material and then sewed together to their shape. Poor Grumio has to find some kind of stretched meaning to justify an attack upon the harassed Tailor.

565. **Though thy little finger be armed in a thimble.** 41,16. The Tailor being a little man and having his little finger thus armed only makes his ' formidable ' quantity more ludicrous.

566. **An I had thee in place where, thou shouldst know it.** 41,17-18. The Tailor may be referring to a law-court.

567. **Then he shall have no odds.** 41,21-2. No chance of sparing Grumio. Grumio has just told the Tailor not to spare him in the conflict, but having taken the Tailor's only weapon (his mete-yard) away from him and given him the bill, the Tailor certainly would not be in a position to spare Grumio. It is a quibble meaning (a) that he won't spare Grumio, (b) that the unarmed man will not be able to think of sparing the other; he cannot help but spare him because he has nothing to hit with.

COMMENTARY

PART II Scene IV

This scene is plain sailing enough not to demand very much detailed commentary. Keep the characters alive especially in the opening episodes. The Pedant, now thoroughly assured of himself, is quite genial and looking forward to his little adventure. The dialogue between Tranio and Biondello is brisk and clinching, Biondello

F*

pointing his message to Baptista with precision to show exactly what he had said.

The Pedant delivers his speech to Baptista with the emphasis which comes from careful instruction, at a moderate and deliberate pace, omitting nothing, and perfectly at his ease. Baptista, noting the Pedant's closely contained speech, praises its shortness and plainness and proceeds happily and courteously to agree to the bargain proposed. The remainder of this passage until the exit offers no difficulty. But keep it interesting as though something is ' toward '. TRANIO is engineering it, BAPTISTA is preparing for it and the action is lively in its modified way.

The final colloquy between LUCENTIO and BIONDELLO is taken quickly, where what was ' toward ' is now more ' toward ' still. The young LUCENTIO is excited about events and the highly exhilarated BIONDELLO, sharp of wit and humour, informs the other of the facts in a slightly fantastic, precise and elaborate way, deliberately adopted

and delivered with a concealed sense of gratification. The nature of this effect is not of any great proportions, but comes from BIONDELLO's curiously alive and slightly odd temperament, and it enables a purely essential piece of plot transaction to assume an attractive modelling and not remain just a dry necessity. At " *I cannot tarry* " he is just about to run off, but comes back, and amusedly, delicately, and speedily delivers himself of the adventure of the lady. After this he is about to go again and then returns and delivers himself of his final piece of information with skipping spirit, ending with his precise and pointed " *to come against* you *come* . . ." and his final singular use of the word ' *appendix* '.

GLOSSARY OF WORDS

568. Pegasus. 42,13. The name of an inn. There was an inn of this name in Cheapside, at this period.

569. Austerity. 42,15. Reserve and dignity; adopt. from OFr.–Lat.–Gk. meaning ' making the tongue dry and rough ' hence ' harsh, severe '.

570. Father. 42,15. See note 505.

571. School'd. 42,18. Instructed as to what he has to do.

572. Tall. 42,26. See note 437.

573. Patrimony. 42,31. The gift of wealth

or property made by a father to his son; Lat. meaning ' that which proceeds from the father '.

574. Bestow'd. 43,3. Disposed of.

575. Curious. 43,4. See note 548.

576. Dissemble. 43,10. See note 195.

577. Dower. 43,13. See note 94.

578. Affied. 43,17. Affianced, betrothed.

579. Assurance. 43,17. See note 283.

580. Scrivener. 43,27. Scribe; adopt. (in aphetic form) from OFr. *escrivain* Lat. *scriba* scribe.

581. Pittance. 43,29. ' A thin and slender pittance '. Frugal hospitality in the way of food and drink.

582. Dally. 43,36. ' Dally not with the gods '. Waste no time talking about the gods.

583. Mess. 43,38. A simple course of food.

584. Counterfeit assurance. 44,4–5. A false bargain because the Pedant is a false Vincentio.

585. Appendix. 44,15. Bianca, the one who is ' attached ' to Lucentio.

GLOSSARY OF PHRASES

586. Set your countenance, sir. 42,27. Look serious. Biondello has just been given some money with which to buy a drink, hence this injunction.

587. Pitchers have ears. 43,20. A proverb warning people to be careful of unsuspected eavesdroppers.

588. We will better it in Pisa. 43,39. We will give Baptista better entertainment when he comes to Pisa.

589. Cum privilegio ad imprimendum solum. 44,5–6. With exclusive copyright, fig. with reference to marriage-rights.

COMMENTARY

PART II SCENE V

KATHARINA is now completely ' tamed ', willing and ready to yield to her husband in any whim that he inflicts upon her. We witness this in this scene. She is gracious and agreeable, and her correction to her husband's ' mistake ' is quite normal and kind. She ultimately agrees with him in his re-adjustment of his wish to call the sun by its proper name and then submits herself in all content to perpetual obedience to his will and wishes.

The following incident carries out this complete change of spirit : PETRUCHIO with characteristically easy humour ' creates ' a ' gentle mistress ' out of the old VINCENTIO. It is delicately elaborated

and addressed with highly pleased appreciation of a charming young girl. KATHARINA obediently follows in his style only to be corrected by PETRUCHIO with assumed ' wonder ' at her mistake. She then gets out of her difficulty without any display of annoyance, and so we are amusingly assured of her complete conversion into a normal and sweetly tempered young woman.

The remainder of the scene is straightforward. It is taken pleasantly and in a lively manner and concludes with HORTENSIO's bold determination to follow PETRUCHIO's example with regard to his own wife, if the need should arise.

GLOSSARY OF WORDS

590. List. 44,27. See note 365.

591. Rush-candle. 44,34. A rushlight made by dipping the pith of a rush in tallow or grease.

592. Bowl. 44,45. The ball used in the game of bowls.

593. A'. 45,9. ' A' will make the man mad '. He; of early dialectal origin and subsequently used by 16th and 17th c.

dramatists to denote familiarity of speech.

594. Favourable stars. 45,13. The ancient belief that the stars influenced human affairs.

595. Reverend. 45,21. ' A reverend father '. The elderly were regarded with respect and reverence.

596. Esteem. 45,38. ' She is of good es-

teem '. Regarded with good esteem by others.

597. Dowry. 45,39. See note 94.

598. Qualified. 45,40. Nobly minded.

599. Jealous. 45,50. Doubtful, cautious.

600. Untoward. 45,53. Unbending, responding only in the same disciplinary manner as Petruchio has effected towards Katharina.

GLOSSARY OF PHRASES

601. **And not unluckily against the bias.** 44,46. In the game of bowls, the actual bowl is so shaped as to cause it to move in a slightly oblique line. Formerly this bias was caused by loading the bowl with lead on one side. If not thrown skilfully it would miss the aim.

COMMENTARY

PART II   SCENE VI

The main plot of the play, the process of taming KATHARINA, having now been accomplished, the sub-plot, or plots, are now brought into action with full force in order to supply the interest, and vigorous action takes the stage once again. The characters concerned are all very well defined and markedly accentuated by their slightly eccentric natures. After the opening incidents, the first of which is swift, secret and urgent, and PETRUCHIO's pleasant colloquy with VINCENTIO, the PEDANT appears at the window in answer to the knock on the door. Incidentally, sounds of revelry, and a chorus lustily sung, should be heard from within the house from the rise of the curtain, at first somewhat subdued and then rising as PETRUCHIO and the others appear. As the wine is freely flowing, the PEDANT is now in a state of intoxication. This makes him bold and even aggressive in his treatment, and enables him to supply an amusing quality to his lines.

BIONDELLO runs on, thoroughly pleased with the successful accomplishment of the marriage between LUCENTIO and BIANCA, and then suddenly gets a big shock and tries to slip away. Make this change as evident as possible. It is action,

amusing action, and must be registered and not thrown away. Tackled by the irate VINCENTIO, he roundly denies his own identity and that of VINCENTIO. This must also be done with fullness of style.

TRANIO's bold appearance and manner is likewise fully maintained throughout this entire episode. He speaks with full confidence in himself and brazens out his imposture to which the outraged VINCENTIO reacts with the utmost vigour. This scene must be played for all that it is worth and carried on in the same way as BAPTISTA and GREMIO take a hand in it. Keep the conflict alive with amusing intensity.

Likewise in the following episode, do not drop the required volume of treatment. It does not require any detailed reference to its dialogue, because the movement of the action is elementary, and simply means an application of earnestness to its development.

The final one is just a short, charming re-issue of PETRUCHIO's authority over his wife, and after the vigour and sharp battle of the preceding chapters of the scene, rounds it off with a due finish created out of the main theme of the play.

GLOSSARY OF WORDS

602. **Cozen.** 46,32. See note 413.
603. **Countenance.** 46,33. See note 114.
604. **Crack-hemp.** 47,4. Lit. one who hangs at the end of a hempen rope, a condemned criminal. Here used as a term of contempt.
605. **Choose.** 47,5. 'I hope I may choose, sir '. He hopes he may have his own opinion about being a crack-hemp.
606. **Copatain.** 47,23. A hat with a tall sugar-loaf crown and narrow brim. The origin of the word is obscure.
607. **Ancient.** 47,28. Old-fashioned and therefore well-mannered.
608. **Habit.** 47,28. ' You seem a sober

ancient gentleman by your habit '. Adopt. from OFr.–Lat. *habére* to have, *reflexively* to be constituted, to be. The meanings have developed from ' holding ' or ' having ', ' haviour ', hence the manner of bearing oneself— the way or condition in which one exhibits oneself (*a*) externally, hence bearing, outward appearance, clothing, (*b*) internally, i.e. inward mental condition, character (habit) of thought and deed.

609. **Cony-catched.** 48,3. See note 440.
610. **Haled.** 48,10. Lit. drawn, hence to

drag about violently, molest, interfere with.
611. **Counterfeit supposes.** 48,22. False suppositions, the Pedant's impersonation of Vincentio.
612. **Blear'd.** 48,22. Lit. made the eyes watery so that they could not see distinctly. The origin of the word, an epithet for the eyes, is uncertain.
613. **Eyne.** 48,22. The older plural form of ' eyes '.
614. **Packing.** 48,23. Secret scheming. The origin is obscure. The meaning is now obsolete.
615. **Countenance.** 48,30. See note 114.

GLOSSARY OF PHRASES

616. **Church o' your back.** 46,4. Church on your back, at your back, behind you; the marriage accomplished.
617. **God send 'em good shipping!** 47,1–2. Good fortune.

618. **My cake is dough.** 48,43. See note 126.
619. **For never-too-late.** 49,4. Yet never . . . (for it is never too late to kiss).

COMMENTARY

PART II   SCENE VII

This final scene of the play contains the happy robustiousness of its predecessors. Everybody is happy. They have had a good supper and now

are seated round the banquet or little supper, quaffing wine and munching fruit, and in high spirits.

The repartee on page 50 must be given with quick clean cut and thrust, with the widow cool and collected and making her points with deliberateness. Then comes a slight swift exchange with KATHARINA—" *A very mean meaning . . .*" which the men take up with instant spirit. Thus the scene proceeds until the wagers are laid on the wives with snap and vigour, and BIONDELLO's return from the first two with their answers greeted with loud laughter. His method of conveying these messages expresses his own personal appreciation of their implications.

Now whereas LUCENTIO and HORTENSIO in giving their instructions to BIONDELLO have done so in quite an ordinary way, when PETRUCHIO instructs GRUMIO to go to *his* mistress, it is with an authoritative " *Sirrah Grumio* ", pause, " *Go to your mistress* ", pause, " *Say* ", pause, " *I command her to come* ", in steady meaning tones, hitting the word *command*.

There is nothing to offer any difficulty in what remains of the scene. It speaks for itself. KATHARINA's last speech to the temperamental women is that of authority graced with kindliness, and pointed with very precise understanding. One feels the big mind and the big heart working together; and there is nothing left for anyone else to say about the duties of a wife to her husband and the husband's wide worthiness which commands his wife's obedience.

GLOSSARY OF WORDS

620. **Afeard.** 49,21. ' Never trust me, if I be afeard '. The Widow uses Petruchio's sense of the word ' fear ' in the preceding line when he says that ' Hortensio fears his widow ' as a means of saying that Hortensio has no power to make her afraid of him, the verb being used transitively.

621. **Roundly.** 50,2. ' Roundly replied '. The reply complete, fully answering the situation. Petruchio takes it as meaning that Hortensio is foolish and making a mistake.

622. **Shrew.** 50,10. See note 103.

623. **Butt.** 50,22. Fight head to head.

624. **Hasty-witted body.** 50,23. A rash or jealous-minded person.

625. **Awaken'd.** 50,25. ' Hath that awaken'd you ? ' Made her alert to any possibilities.

626. **Frighted.** 50,26. ' But not frighted me '. She trusts herself to remain faithful to her husband.

627. **Bird.** 50,29. Target for Petruchio's wit.

628. **Shift my bush.** 50,29. Move away from him.

629. **Prevented.** 50,32. ' She hath prevented me '. Anticipated Petruchio's shaft of wit; lit. come before. This meaning is now obsolete and has become extended to the meaning of ' hindered, frustrated '.

630. **Slipp'd.** 50,35. Released.

631. **Simile.** 50,37. A comparison by likeness; Lat. *simile* neuter of *similis* like.

632. **Currish.** 50,37. A play upon the word; (*a*) of the nature of a cur, (*b*) because he has used the simile of a dog. It is also a jocular intimation that Tranio is more cur than greyhound.

633. **Gird.** 50,41. Sharp biting retort. The origin is obscure. Tranio hits back for the ' currish ' gibe.

634. **A'.** 50,43. See note 593.

635. **Gall'd.** 50,43. Chafed, broken skin.

636. **Crowns.** 50,54. See note 141.

637. **Holidame.** 51,38. A later form of ' halidom ', holiness, sanctity, popularly used as an oath signifying a creature of God. The adoption of ' dam ' for ' dom ' was due to popular etymology in falsely deriving the suffix as from Our Lady. ' Dom ' means ' condition, state of being '.

638. **Swinge.** 51,43. Beat, flay, whip, thrash. It is a later form of ' swenge ', OE. *swengan* to shake, shatter.

639. **Bodes.** 52,1. Signifies; OE. *bodian* from *boda* messenger.

640. **Awful.** 52,3. ' An awful rule '. Rule or authority commanding respect.

641. **Right.** 52,3. ' Right supremacy '. The supremacy of proper things, the husband over the wife.

642. **Dowry.** 52,8. See note 94.

643. **Froward.** 52,13. See note 84.

644. **Bauble.** 52,16. See note 528.

645. **Bandy.** 53,13. Throw as a ball, backwards and forwards.

646. **Vail.** 53,17. ' Vail your stomach '. Lower her pride; adopt. from OFr. *valer* or an aphetic form of *avaler* to lower.

647. **Boot.** 53,17. Good, profit; OE. *bót* good, useful.

648. **Toward.** 53,24. ' When children are toward '. Obediently minded, disposed towards good behaviour.

GLOSSARY OF PHRASES

649. **My banquet is to close our stomachs up.** 49,13. This light repast is simply to round off the principal meal. The context appropriates this meaning which was quite common together with the more familiar one of a ' sumptuous meal '.

650. **He that is giddy thinks the world turns round.** 50,1. Katharina explains what she means two speeches later.

651. **Thus I conceive by him.** 50,4. She answers according to what Petruchio has said. ' Conceive ' lit. means ' to take effectively, take to oneself, take in and hold '. The uterine sense arises as a result of the taking of seed from the male by the female and thus forming a new body. Hence conception of idea or bearing.

652. **Conceives by me !** 50,5. Petruchio uses the other meaning of the word, namely ' conceives a child '.

653. **Thus she conceives her tale.** 50,6. That is how she comes to make her statement.

654. **My Kate does put her down.** 50,18. Kate will get the better of her, subdue her.

655. **That's my office.** 50,19. That is Hortensio's function as the Widow's husband.

656. **Spoke like an officer.** 50,20. Like one who will do the office in another's (Katharina's) stead.

657. **Your head and butt were head and horn.** 50,24. This refers to Gremio's remark about fighting head to head. As in the first speeches at the top of the page there has been a jesting allusion to the Widow having a child by Petruchio; this is now used by Bianca to imply that unless the people concerned were not easily suspicious, Hortensio might be threatened with cuckoldry, that is the condition of a husband deceived by his wife, and therefore one who was jocularly supposed to grow horns. Bianca alludes to the ' butting ' as between stags.

658. **'Tis thought your deer does hold you at a bay.** 50,39. Tranio tells Petruchio that it is a good job that nobody wooed Katharina in his place, because it is believed that she keeps him at a distance and will not obey him. ' To hold or keep at a bay ' was the action of a hunted animal successfully warding off its pursuers. The two words ' a bay ' are also a pun on ' obey '. The suggestion is that she may have someone else that she loves and thus Petruchio is in danger of becoming a cuckold.

659. **Hath he not hit you here ?** 50,42. Pointing to his forehead (where the ' horns ' may grow).

660. **And as the jest did glance away from me.** 50,44. As the jest did not really apply to him, because Katharina was faithful.

661. **'Tis ten to one it maim'd you two outright.** 50,45. Their butting hurt themselves more than it hurt Petruchio.

662. **And, to be short, what not, that's sweet and happy.** 52,4. And in short, what is not, but what is sweet and happy.

663. **I would your duty were as foolish too.** 52,20. Bianca has just told her husband that she thinks his action in trying to get her foolishly to comply with her duty was a very foolish thing to do. He replies that he only wishes that her sense of duty had the foolishness of wisdom, i.e. the wisdom of bending obediently to rightful authority and not trying to look so independent and strong-minded. It requires an accent on the word ' foolish '.

664. **The more fool you, for laying on my duty.** 52,23. Bianca tells Lucentio that it was stupid of him to take her duty for granted, ' laying ' meaning ' wagering '.

665. **We three are married, but you two are sped.** 53,27. Petruchio tells Lucentio and Hortensio that they are all three married men, but he is successful and prosperous in happiness whilst they are already at variance with theirs.

666. **Though you hit the white.** 53,28. The white was the centre mark on the practice target in archery.

COMMENTARY

PART II   SCENE VIII (EPILOGUE)

This obviously is not Shakespeare; its crudity proclaims that. SLY gradually wakes up and takes full time to do so. When the HOSTESS informs him sharply that his wife will curse him for his absence, he feels quite sure that he will know how to handle such a contingency and measures out his reply very precisely. He, like Bottom, has had a 'rare dream' and he makes this apparent. Then he determines to go and change his learning into teaching with a relish that we feel would provide the good substance for another play.

GLOSSARY OF WORDS

667. **Bravest.** 54,1. 'I have had The bravest dream tonight'. Because he was elevated into the brave or noble condition of being a lord.

GLOSSARY OF PHRASES

668. **A lord with a mission.** 53,41. A lord with a journey in front of him. He has got to go away from where he is.

INDEX